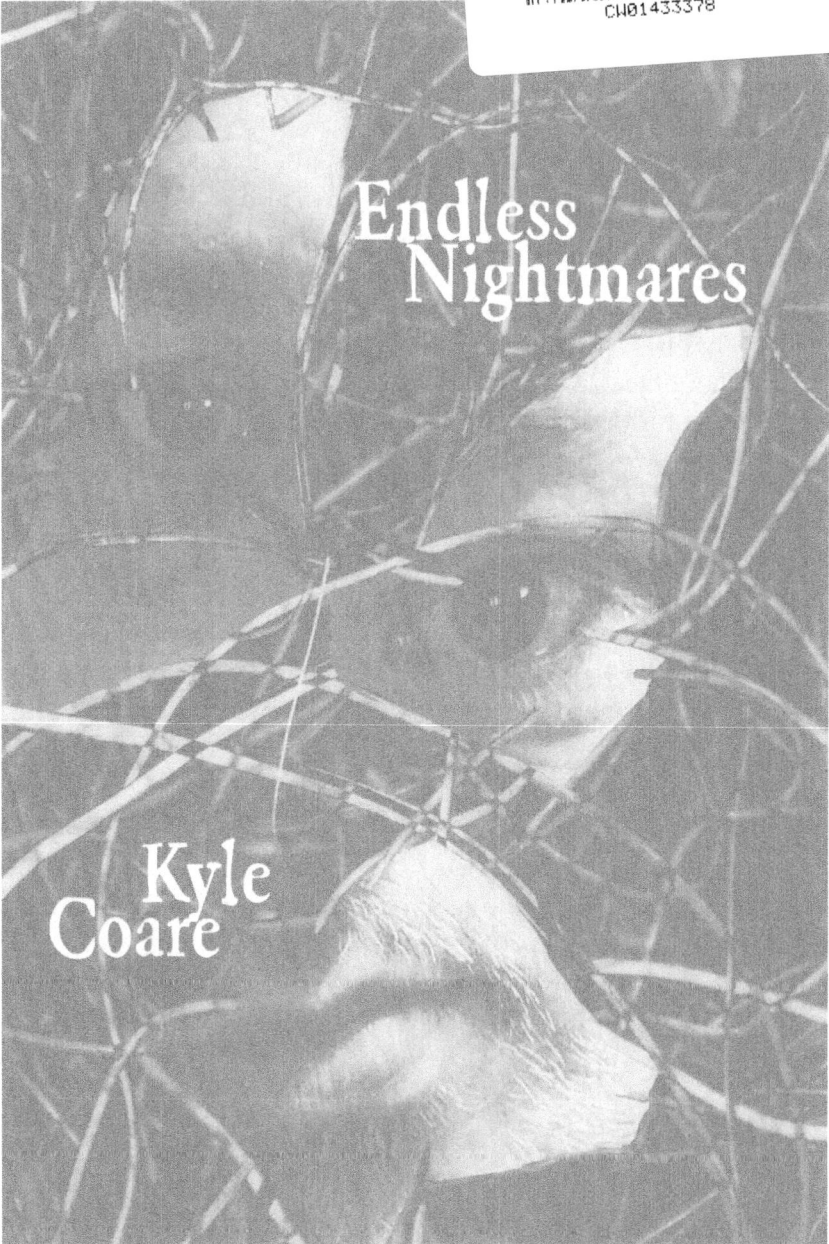

Endless Nightmares

Kyle Coare

Endless Nightmares

Kyle Coare

Other works by Kyle Coare.

Poetry

Prisoner of The Mind
(ISBN 978-1722975944)

Prisoner of The Heart
(ISBN 978-1731442475)

The Night Watchman
(ISBN 978-1797484419)

Seasons
(ISBN 978-1689340434)

Lone Wolf
(ISBN 979-8613023912)

Headfirst into the storm
(ISBN 979-8526622288)

In Shadows
(ISBN 979-8448585333)

Torn Pages: Scraps of midnight
(ISBN 979-8375840512)

Non-Fiction

A Brief History of Video Games
(ISBN 979-8391983460)

All available from Amazon in both Paperback and Kindle Edition

Table of Contents

Acknowledgements v

ONE 7

Endless nightmares 8
Unscathed 10
Scary dreams 12
At night 15
3am thoughts 16
Grind 18
Haunted 20
Black dress 22
Chalk outlines 24
Insidious eyes 26
A ghost is born 28
The hum returns 30
Subway lights 32
Eternal love 34
Sky cries oceans 35
The Anti-muse 36
Creeping death 38
Corridors 40
Gargantuan 42
Children of ze night 44
Ghost house 45
The watchman stands 46
Stale 48
Quiet 50
Morsels 52
Lighthouse 54
Creepy hotel 56
Angels guiding 58
False hope 60
Eyes of moonlight 62
HellHeaven 64
Feel 66
Out of time 68
Cravings 70
A place called nowhere 72
Answers 74
My shadow 76
Hounded 77

TWO.. 79

A cup of tea in Hell 80
Dreams & nightmares... 82
One hell of an open mic 84
The walk of lost hope 86
The hum grows 87
Deja vu.. 88
Forever in shade 90
I hear them 92
In too deep 94
Ghost stories 96
Late... 98
Ink... 100
Blanket of night 102
Snaps 104
Stage... 106
Phantom words 108
Well 110
On the wisp of the wind 112
Remembrance 114
Empty, endless streets 116
Listen 118
A single shot 120
Inner voice.. 121
Mental fog 122
Locked 124
Name the ghosts 126
Lies 128
Demonic dance 130
Ghostly patrol... 132
Bus stop 134
Losing sleep 136
Arecibo 137
When night falls the watchman calls.................................. 138
Last orders.. 140
Red lights 142
Curse... 144

THREE 147

The stopped clock 148
My life as a blood sucking beast of the night.................150
Winter song 152
Stuck in grey...154
Traffic...156
Under strobing streetlight 158
Trial of the watchman...160
Midnight blue eyes 162
Monday...164
Midnight sludge 166
Distorted replica 168
Is there anyone out there? 170
Bottled 172
The importance of contact..174
Opening a window 177
Squirms 178
Hope is gone 180
Out of time 2..182
Mothman 184
Ghosts of history...185
Murmured name..186
Tomb...188
Oozing 190
Life flows...192
Breath on a mirror 194
The flow of time..195
Pain 196
Surge of hate...198
Old hat 200
Prison island..202
Shattered hope 204
Black Widow 206
Meat grinder..208
Ghost of romance 210
Foul entities 212
Mourning song...214
Out of the box..216
Downpour alley..219

FOUR 221

Maze 222
Shadow world 224
Book of memories 226
Cascading diamonds 228
Burnt visions 230
Hall of mirrors 232
Our ghosts follow 234
Machine 236
Shyness 238
A vision of hope 240
Shards 241
Artificial 242
Ghost of love 244
Pulled trigger 246
Silence 248
Teething 250
The last bus 252
Woman in black 254
Traveller 256
Twist of reality 258
White sheet 260
Wrung out 262
Instruction book 264
Impact 266
Rise of the anti-muse 268
Altar 270
Fool's gold 272
Snake 274
Anxiety bomb 275
Forest 276
Head in a vice 278
Darkness consumes 281
Monsters 282
Webs 284
Lifted 287
Weathered 288
Dues paid 290
ABOUT THE AUTHOR 299

Acknowledgements

This book has been a long process. Without the amazing support from friends and family, I don't know if I could have completed it.

To my mum, and my brother, you have listened to me, advised me, guided me, ensured I ate when all I could concentrate on was my work!

To my fellow poets and spoken word artists, every time I see or hear your poems or stories it inspires me to keep going.

To those that host nights, like Sammy at Some-Antics, Samantha at Get Mouthy, you have given us a place to share our words our thoughts and to feel a part of something, and I truly thank you for that.

To all the people that read my work, buy my books, watch me perform, you are all so important, without all of you my words would just be me shouting at the air.

To those that are no longer with us, I will always miss you, but you will live on in the words.

Peace, Love and Poetry.
Kyle

ONE

**The darkness that surged
through men's hearts
was only the start.
A mere trick to get
wicked words to trickle freely
from crooked lips.
Now into this
nightmare reality we slip.**

Endless nightmares

What we thought
we left
in shadows,
was never really gone.
Things pushed
to the darkest parts.
Their terror
carried on.

What we had
coming,
was only
the beginning.
The darkest nights
were soon
to be
All
that we
would be
seeing.

The things
hiding
in the dark,
They were
merely spies
Keeping
watch
Through
beady
little eyes.

The true terror
lurks further
behind
and now it's hungry
for flesh.
Coming to grind
any bones it finds
and build
itself a nest.

What we thought
we left
in shadows,
was merely
a preview.
Now the true terror
sees you,
and into dreams
he seeps through
as you sleep.
Bringing
endless nightmares
and terror
that will make
your brain
feel weak.

Unscathed

Take my hand,
let it lead you
through this
nightmare world.
Let it guide, on this
spooky ghost train
ride. Let it hold
your hand. Tight.
As the fear starts to bite,
let it ease away the fright
as we stumble through
this cavernous
world of the night.

Take my hand,
and we will explore
this upside-down land
as the visions and apparitions
try to grip around your feet,
from deep in the claggy quicksand.
Fingers jammed
in ears,
to withstand the screams,
whistling from fanged creatures
of the damned.
In this terrifying dream.

Take my hand
as we run through
this maze of scares,
creepy staircase of fears,
where the surface bubbles
under its own breath
and the air is stagnant
with the pungent scent of death.

But don't be afraid.
This hand won't let go,
it won't run away.
It will hold on tight.
as the crazed beings
rise from their graves.
It will hold on
to make sure
you come out
of the other side
unscathed.

Scary dreams

On darkened tides,
endless nightmares,
scary dream rides.
On open roads,
up mountains high.
Nowhere to hide
from the terrors he finds.
The many visions projected
upon his stuttering film screen mind

Endless nightmares
and open roads.
Too many dark tales told.
Countless games played for his soul.
Could someone pray
for this poor mortal's wellbeing?
Because ghosts and monsters
are all he is seeing.
Now he has nowhere else to go,
but back into hell
to pay his due.

Listened to so many
wretched nightmare sounds,
as they oozed deep
into his ear canals.
Tarring every part
with their screams
and orchestrations
of being pulled apart.

Fretted over too many noises.
Screeching voices
that were hidden between
the drifting, flowing drapes of reality
and the eternally shifting seas
of the other side.
Heard the living
and the dead
walking beside.
Now he has to grab his coat
and run, flee, and hide

Endless nightmares
of open roads.
Where the horizon
never gets any closer,
just another fiction told.
You just keep on travelling
as the places get further.
The destination never becomes clearer,
you never get any nearer,

Through the distorted lens
of this tangled
abstract substantiality.
The gleaming skyscrapers you see.
Just twisted mirages
of this warped reality.
Across the blistered desert
of your fractured stuttering sanity.

Have walked along these
nightmare roads into hell
for so long, I've sailed the
hellish seas. The fiery friaries
in this village of the damned.
I've walked the open roads,
felt the hot winds slam.
I've traipsed along these
torturous turns
for many a twisted trial,
along these trails
I travelled alone
and now
this hell,
well
It feels
like home.

At night

There is someone out there,
in the darkness watching.
I hear them rustling but only shadows do I see
There is someone out there,
I sense their eyes staring,
I can feel the looks.
Penetrative and icy to me

There is someone out there,
I can hear their movement
but no shapes
can I spy.
As the moon hides her face
behind clouds.
Nothing,
just the darkness
floating by.

There is someone out there,
as I look into the darkness.
I know they are staring right back at me.
Their figures hidden from view,
their yellowing eyes I don't see
but I hear them,
as you would do too.

There is someone out there.
Just outside my line of sight,
slight flickers of figures darting/
trying to cause me fright.
The way the streetlight casts shadows,
seems to seep right through them.
Even though they are seemingly translucent
to tears they do reduce me.

3am thoughts

Paranoia creeps up on you.
It doesn't startle with a thud,
it's more insidious than that.
Sits inside the mind stirring
a vast vat of overflowing fears,
dripping over your thoughts
until they are all soaked through.

Trapped in a prison
but the walls don't protect.
The feelings they repel
make you feel more under attack.
The paranoia is settling in now.
It has made itself at home,
with a nice mug of cocoa.
Ready to chill you to your bones.

Darkness feeds the paranoia,
gives it room to breathe,
room to think.
That noise.
Just the pipes in the bathroom?
Or my fate?
Walking in with chains that clink.

A bang awakens me.
Was it in my dream or reality?
Hazy images flood my tired mind.
A lone corpse,
its severed head lay beside.

I shake away the thoughts
that prey on my still sleepy brain
and explore,
no bodies on the floor.
For now, at least.
Though the thoughts
are raining for sure
and I feel my fear increase.

I investigate.
Every light on,
knowing that this
will probably seal my fate,
bring forth my doom.
Cost me a fortune,
receiving the electricity bill
will be my ruin.

Nothing unusual, I admit,
heartbeat raised a bit.
Sleep a thing I'll have to forfeit.
The paranoia takes a while to subside.
So, I sit. In my stupidly lit up home
like a Christmas light display.
Now even the shadows cannot roam
but at least there isn't a being hiding near.
I think as the hairs on my neck
prickle up with a strange tingle of fear.
I hear a thud.
this time it is right behind me

I turn.

The lights go out.

Grind

Clanging in the distance,
I can hear it getting closer
like the machinery of death,
it's wheels grinding over.
I hear its heinous screech
as the moon hides
behind clouds for cover.

It's rushing towards me,
I hear its howl.
A roar in the night.
A beast on the prowl.
The pounding thuds,
the clank of chains
dragged across wood.
The sound of squelching mud,
or is that rivers of blood?

I hear it getting louder.
It's starting to drown out
the thoughts in my head.
I hear its aching sound,
mimicking repulsive
voices of the dead.
The mechanical ring
like teeth grinding
right through your jaw lining.
I hear it.
Its inside now.
It's starting to shred.

Now my thoughts don't work.
My legs jelly, my brain aches.
like mental spaghetti.
It's all gone wrong.
I can't take
this torturous
devil song
any longer.
I'm being eaten
from within.
I don't have long.

Please

For the love of God.

Run.

Haunted

My house is haunted
by bad memories and regret.
Conversations I'd rather forget.
Ghosts of times
where things were bad,
These ghosts of mine
just make me feel sad.

Fear seeps through the walls
of this old residence,
when the visitors call
to share their presence.
In the late-night hours
the air sours.

Phantoms roam, screech, and moan
leaving me wearied, worried. Alone?
In rooms locked tight,
keys long buried.
They wail through the night.

Evil within
battered wood
and stone skin.
Scratching
behind the fireplace.
Cold spots
on the creaking staircase,
and the heart
that beats at a frantic pace.

This house. Possessed
by unwanted guests.
They flitter through the walls
until darkness falls,
then they start their assault.
Noisily forcing nerves to take hold.
Then they pull them tighter
like sharp cheese wire,
until my mind is frayed
and my fear is on fire.

In my house I hear the sounds,
during the night they scream so loud.
Their horrifying voices take flight.
There is nowhere to hide.
An unwilling passenger
on a ghost train ride.

This house. So cold,
haunted and old.
It creaks and groans
like old weary bones.
The unwanted ones walk
and with whispered talk,
they remind
of things you don't want to hear,
they are the ones I fear.

This old house creaks.
The energy reeks of fear and despair,
the acrid taste of last night's screams,
the smashed remnants
of yesterday's bad dreams,
scattered in pieces all over the floor.
If I could leave, I'd leave
but in here
there isn't a door.

Black dress

She is the moon to my dark night
adding lightness to guide my path
like a star to my grey cloud,
I'm the thunder roaring loud.
She the lightning that blinds
the glue that binds.
I'm the one always trying
to run and hide,
flee from the feelings
I hold deep inside.

She is the voice
that speaks delicate tones.
I'm the screams that echo
through creaky old bones.
Tread careful weary traveller,
her sign would say,
as I bound towards the edge
and as I sway
ready to fall.
I think.
She would be the hand
that pulls me back from the brink.

She is the voice that sits in my head,
when I'm lying awake in my bed.
She is the one that says
just close your eyes,
don't look around in dread.
I know not her name.
I've never seen her face.
Just felt her sweet embrace.

If I close my eyes
I sometimes catch a glimpse.
A swaying black dress dancing
in the inky blackness
of the vast empty expanse.

I sometimes hear
her voice
on the wind.
When all the other voices
are being unkind.
Is she just a figment
of the mind?
Or is she
a voice from someplace else
trying to send me a sign?

Kyle Coare

Chalk outlines

Chalk
outlines
a body
lain
slain.
Blood stains
the ground.
It pools
all around.
Lived life
selling
white lines.

Lived life
selling high times.
A steep decline.
Missed
a deadline.
Now he's dead,
out of time
at the end of the line.

You can pick the flesh
from the bones
of the story.
A victim
of atrocity.
A victim
of the violent city.

Chalk outlines
the body
on the ground,
Sirens sound,
another turf war
going down.
Chalk outlines
all over town.
Chalked off,
another statistic
In his war-torn
battleground.

Chalk outlines
all that remains
in the dull twilight.
The red stain,
Ink black
in the light
of the weeping satellite.
Lived life
selling fake smiles.
Sirens will wail tonight
through the air
that cries in silent foresight.
Knowing
that chalk outlines
multiply.

Insidious eyes

They are in the trees.
Yellow eyes glaring out,
encircling me.
Everywhere I look
another pair of vicious stares.
Reading me like an open book.
Spin around, take to ground
but you can't escape the snide eyes
that try to drag you down.

They are in the darkness.
In the shadows,
in every nook and cranny.
In every picture book,
everywhere I look.
It's uncanny.
They all stare with such hate.
They all stare,
like I'm a worm used as bait.

Footprints,
so big I could fall in,
6 foot deep,
perfect fit for a coffin.
Precariously
I try to avoid the holes
even as the looming death bell tolls.

Insidious leers they peer inside.
They peek to find the truth I hide,
then twist and distort
to fill my heart with ice.
Circling, they sense fear
I await, shaking away
the shards and spikes.

Where to turn?
Not alone
but I can't see anyone.
I can only feel the static in the air.
Making every single hair pay attention
like they are making
their final preparations.
To run.

I step through this overgrown nightmare,
I feel a presence everywhere,
malevolent it fills the air.
In fear I run.
Run from the lies that burn,
eyes that turn inwards.
They stare, inside my mind,
penetrating the soul I lay bare.

But where can you run?
The woodland only hides
even bigger beasts.
The pathway ahead?
To a dead end you'll be led.
Your best hope
is to pinch yourself
and pray that you
awaken in your bed.

A ghost is born

Every moment another ghost is born.
Torn from living to the lands beyond.
Where they haunt
like memories
of a cold day in December.
Hazy hate-stained reminder
of every floating burning ember.

Every second another ghost is born.
To wonder
where their lives went so wrong.
To look out at the great unknown.
Morose.
With eyes that will no longer close.
Eyelids that are see through,
transparent,
all you see is the cold wet dew.

Every cycle of the moon,
a host of ghosts are born too soon.
To wander lonely
like leaves torn from a tree,
blowing in the breeze.
These newcomers to the other side
need an overseer, a guide,
to help them cope.
The man in black is there
to show them the ropes.

Every second another ghost is born,
ripped from the living
to the land of the gone.
Face pulled tight and forlorn.
Features weary,
ragged and worn.
Screams moulded on face
like wet clay
dripping into another day

Kyle Coare

The hum returns

The hairs on my neck snapped up
like meerkats surveying the scene.
Tingles in my arms,
triggered goosebumps and alarms,
the sense that something was wrong.
A siren song. Calling me to follow along.

The hum was back,

It had returned in a snap.
I Listened to it. I couldn't resist.
The sounds got inside
and started to twist,
slimy roots around my brain.
Branches reaching out
to pull me down again.

Beyond its hypnotic grind,
I listened to the wind. Wild and loud.
In between the sounds,
I thought I was losing my mind,
I heard my own heart start to pound
and screams
trying to escape from my lungs
but from in deep no sounds would come.

I should have stayed inside,
not strayed out into the cold dark night,
but I was enticed by sounds that lied.
Sounds that poked and prodded
somewhere behind my eyelids, closed tight.
I wanted to yell
but who would I tell.
The result would have just been echoed sobs.
I should have run but my feet were heavy
like I was wearing cement coated clogs.

I listened to the hum,
never should have done.
It's indistinct chilling rasping.
Should have clasped
my hands tight over my ears.
It soon filled my head with fear.
It twisted words like hate and anger,
into the forefront of my eyes
and placed words upon my tongue
like vengeful tigers
or wrathful songs
that the devil once sung.

I listened to the hum
and it corrupted every atom.
It sucked clean my goodness
leaving only dirt and scum.
I listened to its sound,
it was like I was found,
at first it was like a choir singing
but soon it morphed
into death bells ringing.

I listened to the hum
and
this is my warning
to you
If you hear it.
Run
as soon as you do.

Subway lights

She rides the subway lights,
has done for years.
Eyes cry, bleached tears
as the brakes screech.
But too late for poor Sally.
The blinding vision
a tunnel of white.
A push in the back
and the world fell out
from beneath her.

Sally rides the subway winds,
the rushing sounds of subway trains.
The strains of screams
in the distance.
She dreams she has wings
and is flying above
the gunmetal rails,
bathed in light
as she took flight.

Sally rides
the subway lights
as they strobe
over dying eyes.
Last sight
she will see this night.
A sad end
to a talented life.
The trains stopped
running
early tonight.

Never hurt anyone in his life,
never knew why,
the voices in his head
screamed she needs to die.
Telling him to push.

He pushed.

His padded cell walls

his head rushed.

Blinded by those

subway lights.

Disgust at his own hands.

Distrust in his own mind.

Distraught at the thoughts

that scream through

like trains of dust

through those

subway lights.

Eternal love

The stone statue
looked
longingly over
at the faded tomb
of her
long lost lover.
Alone.
Forever
she would stand.
Watching.
Waiting.
Forever.
A stony vigil.
No clocks ticking.
A solitary tear
eternally sculpted
to sombre ashen face.
Weathered.
So, the tear
is mostly faded.
Her features
long ago degraded
but her heart
never left
the place
she stood
and waited.

Sky cries oceans

The dreary grey of this autumn day
gives way to the murky moonless night.
Only streetlights and the rare house light
illuminate the streets tonight.
It's way past midnight
and most have retired for the eve.
Taken to their dreams,
only us night owls do they leave.

Listening to the soft trickle,
the delicate tickle of rain
as it hits the window frame
like the sound of stars
twinkling in the sky.
Hitching a ride on the tracks
of a long-forgotten raindrop.
It rolls down the windowpane
before launching itself once more into the air.
Hitting the ground with a barely audible splash.

And then
the heavens open
and the sky cries oceans.
The tears of millions
all fall at once.
The streets below overflow
like rivers gushing, waters rushing
trying to find somewhere to go.

Zombie leaves move once more
animated by the torrential downpour.
Travelling down the gutter lane,
they only stop at the gurgling drains.
The sounds surround in these silent hours,
echoing nature
and her mystic powers.

The Anti-muse

She tries
to confuse,
to make your words obtuse.
Twisting your metaphors
into balls of nothing.
To make your words sit silent
when the sounds should ring.
The anti-muse.
She laughs at the work you do,
points out the flaws in the words you use.
She paces around the room,
stomping feet
thudding
through the silence.

She sits
with sneered lips parted.
Ready to impart
a spear tip of hurried words.
A flurry of verbal put downs,
a series of smearing frowns
and groans, echoing moans,
unhelpful tones.
Eyes roll inside, sighs her despise.
She never offers advice,
just tells you it's no good,
her yawns are never disguised.

She fills the air with tension.
It swirls with stormy apprehension,
screeching in the wind.
She screams through your dreams,
corrupting your sleep,
crushing the peace.
She never lets you rest,
her barbs never cease.

She prods,
asking are you done yet,
why don't you write better,
quicker, wittier,
more that will connect.
Why not give up
or try to write a book,
something else completely.
Take up a different hobby,
this is not the path you seek.
Don't get up on stage and try to speak.
She will make your voice fragile and weak,
call you a freak,
telling you that no one wants
to hear your pained squeaks.
She just wants you to follow the sheep,
try not to be unique.
If you listen to the anti-muse
then the outlook is bleak.

Creeping death

I hear a wretched sound
out on those deathly moors.
I hear a squelching noise,
but my eyes won't adjust,
can't focus
into the creeping mist,
where only
oily shadows exist.

I hear it so close,
like a cut gurgling throat,
choking on the words
that it's trying to impart.
I feel it clinching, clinging
to my cold frozen heart.
Gripping it
and pulling the icicles out,
like fingers tearing petals
from a flower.

I hear it echo.
All around murmurs
almost solid, getting firmer.
Terror played
in surround sound.
I can't move,
feet have grown roots.
Entangled with
the very earth itself.
The shadows dance.
Encircling,
they twirl around.
Menacing.

I hear it.

Then I realise,

I've heard it before

On long nights, alone,

I've heard it's rageful roar.

I've felt fear claw

as it paws at my door.

The palpitations,

the shortness of breath,

I've met them many a time

Anxiety can feel

like a slow creeping death

when you are at the end of the line.

Corridors

Running down
twisting,
spiral passages.
Nauseating
treacle covered corridors.
Feet sticking,
sucked into the floor.
Disorientating shadows,
send me spinning,
seems like the demons
are winning
and they are coming back for more.

Try to talk but my voice
feels muddy,
cloying and stuck
like I have a hair caught
within my throat
It comes out in an echoing,
contorted choke.
Distant and distorted
like it's in another room,
covered and hidden,
walled up and boarded.
To stop it being heard
through the gloom.

The clocks are
spinning wildly
clockface dripping,
hands waving frantically.
Time makes no sense it seems.
It's crawling after me now,
with ferocious teeth and a vicious growl.
The place falling to pieces at the seams.

Things are happening
out of order,
I'm in a room,
then I'm not.
I'm finding It hard
to follow the plot.
My vision is melting
in front of me
like recollections
of soon forgotten dreams.

The demon awaits.
Standing 50 feet high
in front of fiery gates.
He points my way in
and into dust he evaporates
but instead of a fire filled world
I awake from the nightmare
into my own bed.
My clothes smell of sulphur
and sweat drips
from my sooty head.

Kyle Coare

Gargantuan

Turbulent seas.
Beneath the waves
gargantuan beings.
Hidden from light,
avoiding all life,
sitting silent,
biding their time,
hurting nobody.
Under turbulent seas
leviathan sleeps.

Drills
disturb the peace.
Drills
damage the beast,
awaken him
from peaceful dreams,
from soft warm sleep.

Angry,
he sees plastic bags
and human faeces,
nets trapping fishes,
plastic rings choking life,
coke can floating by.
Under turbulent seas,
now frothing,
raging, angry waves,
crashing.
Tearing at the beach.

Shoreline sands
devoured.
Water soured.
Oil flow fountains
mixed with blood
for hundreds of miles.
The colossal beast
from a land
of coral reefs,
feasts
on humankind.
Savouring
every morsel he can find.
Then sinks low beneath the waves,
into the seabed duvet,
and closes his eyes
for some peace at last.

The beast sleeps.

No nets are cast.

Children of ze night

People can come at me
with their sticks and torches
but hey, I have a castle,
with a drawbridge.
It's nice, if a little draughty.
I sleep all day,
at night I seek food.
A teenager you say?
Nay I have lived more years
than my human appearance betrays.

I have friends that buck most trends.
Bryan down the way is a man by day
and by night, howls he sends
baying for blood
into the pale moonlight.
He likes to grow his hair,
only once a month though,
but my,
on that night it does truly flow.

There is Joan,
the grey lady that walks my home
She doesn't say a lot, just a wispy moan
that chills all of my visitors to the bone.
She sweeps through the rooms, through the walls too.
Not an obstacle
when you are a ghoul

But back to me, it's time for tea
I like mine body temperature.
Straight from the neck,
warm soothing and red
Oozing, pooling down my throat,
I bleed them till they are dead.

Ghost house

This is the ghost house.
Where terrifying dreams
drift through the walls.
Chains rattle and break
when darkness falls.
It's a place where your last breath is gurgled,
where you feel encircled by those blinking eyes.
It's the place
where you are fated to die.

This is the ghost house.
Your final resting place,
where nightmares chase,
breaking through sleep's peaceful embrace.
Where the chattering of skeletal voices
clatter through the grinding, humming noises.

Nightmares are sowed,
seeds of horror grow.
Seas of dread flow,
in this place where terror
is your only bedfellow.

This is the ghost house.
Try to outrun the guttural breathing.
Cover your ears to protect yourself.
It won't help.
The walls are bleeding.
Hide beneath the covers,
the duvet your sanctuary
but not today.
This place will be the death of you
and you will become one of the hosts,
another ghost roaming these rooms.
Luring others to their fateful tombs.

The watchman stands

The watchman looks
over long forgotten skies.
Time had slowly crept past,
since he had looked out last
upon this city so vast.
Enshrouded by love,
he had started to give up.
Shaped in mystery,
shaded in moonlight.
He had taken a break.
but now the darkness
beckoned him back for the fight.
The demons were lurking
in the fog that fell
upon the city of the night.

Weary bones ache,
too long since this concrete
had reverberated through
his pounding feet.
every foot fall, A sharp stabbing
like ice-cold fingers grabbing hot veins.
Every strained step.
enflamed muscles
that had grown old
through misuse and neglect,
but he kept marching.
Knowing deep inside
that the demons were watching.

On his hunched back
his old guitar,
battered and cracked
with strings missing,
but even now its mystic music sings.
The demons hate this thing,
this instrument of pain,
makes their heads sting.
The dream thieves never see him coming
but they know he is near,
when they hear
his guitar strumming.

Through gritted worn-down teeth,
he hums a refrain,
something he'd heard
deep in the world beneath
and he forgot about his pain.
Took to the city like a steam train,
walking every street,
every alley and darkened underpass.
He kept the sleep depriving demons at bay
He shut out the nightmare
inducing creeps along the way.
The thieves that steal
the dreams of the weak and feeble.
He sealed away
and he sat.
Letting his guitar gently play.
His work over
at least for today,

Stale

The agonised wheezing
and grinding of bones.
The awful tones
of those wretched moans.
The sound that comes
when the hum has dulled,
when darkness falls,
the voices from beyond
start to call.

The aching weight
that fills the air,
old decrepit building
that fills this nightmare.
The lair
where
demons appear,
where fear
is your only friend
and it's standing near,
just a step behind you,
until the end.

The rancid stench
like decomposing skin,
fills the air like gas in an airtight room.
Your breath starts to thin,
then like a match is struck. *BOOM.*
You are in pieces.
Your mind scattered into the breeze.
The fear increases.
It circles as you turn to catch a sight,
it fills your mind
with eternal night.

You can feel its stale breath,
smell the rotten scent of death.
Decay is all that is left
in this place
where sunlight is bereft.
Nothing good can come from these parts,
just the sullen echoes of broken hearts.
Where the dead walk the lands
just wishing to depart.

Quiet

It's gotten a little quiet of late.
We used to have to tempt people
through these creaking gates
but now it seems our services
are no longer required/
I used to be the prince of darkness I should state.
My worker demons no longer needed,
the world has been seeded with hate.

We used to rely on trickery
but now it seems the people
have it down to a tee.
No longer do we need
to make them envious,
they are already so full of greed.

It's gotten a tad flat,
boring and old hat.
I used to enjoy my work.
Hanging around at the crossroads after midnight,
playing my fiddle,
to get another soul to sign.
But now they give away their souls all of the time
on Facebook...
for free.
No autographs for me.

I used to be the purveyor of division,
now I'm seen
as just another parlour magician.
True division
is caused by the suits,
the politicians
and It's getting terribly crowded in here.
Those rowdy Etonians
take up a lot of space I fear

I used to be
the master of ceremonies
but I have nothing
on those tory cronies.
Their parties
are quite legendary.
Dancing and fighting
whilst the population
is on its knees.
Pissed up,
and throwing up in the gutter,
they do as they please.

I used to have power,
now I'm just another service provider
and I think some of those guys
are eying up my job.
We used to take pride
in every soul we took,
now it's harder
to turn them away.
I need a holiday.
Somewhere far away from here.
Just me, some sand,
and a nice cold beer.

Morsels

On these lonely tides
after midnight has been and gone,
I sit in darkness.
Just listening to the internal song,
the sounds of my story,
bubbling under the surface.
The pain inside, did I deserve this?
For wanting to love.
For wanting to live.
For being shy, for being me.
For wanting to give.
Was it all you hoped it would be?
Breaking my will,
making me fall, leaving me still.
Was it worth the pain?
To feel my hope build up
then collapse again.

In twisted vines of history,
you find lines of my story.
The hurt, the pain, the betrayal.
All tangled in those roots,
I watched my life stolen,
I built four walls
to hide the rest of my loot.
I should have died,
but was saved,
I watched my own colour fade,
my energy drain.
I saw myself in blue shades,
a corpse-like stain
on this world of rage.

From the strands and threads that spin in the air,
swirling cobwebs of hurt and despair,
I pluck fly sized morsels of my history,
I place them in a notepad, to tell my story.
All the moments I was made to feel bad,
all the lies that were flooding my head,
all the grinding words that you said,
all the ways you twisted the screw.
All the ways I trusted you.
All the ways the world kept me down.
All the times it kicked and kicked,
it thought it had me licked
but out of the darkness
a beacon was lit
and I walked
head held high
towards it.

Lighthouse

The thunderous rushing
of ravenous waves,
hungrily devouring those
that get in the way.
The tidal assault keeps crashing.
Foamy seas churning,
Angry, they spray the air.
The old building stands there.
Walls crumbling
under sea-salt barrage.

The lighthouse door
opens with a click,
empty it seems,
not a sound inside,
though the air
feels thick.
Eerily quiet,
just the muffled sound
of waves against stone
and the quiet intake
of his breath. Alone.
It bounces
from the walls,
the wooden beams.
It echoes
up the stairway.
The spiral that he'd seen
in his most fearful dreams.

Footsteps on cold stone,
hit with a slap, the sound
not too dissimilar in tone
to that of a thunderclap.
He takes the steps
one by one.
Slowly.
He has seen this place
in so many dreams.
"Nightmares."
The voice in his head screams
as his heart starts to pace.

The treacherous stone,
slippery and wet.
The shivery thoughts
slip through his head.
Roof leaking.
It drips, drips, drips.
He reaches the top
and from the inky backdrop,
that gurgled moan,
previously just a nightly drone.
Now rumbles through
his shattering bones,
as he tumbles down
these crumbling stones.
His neck snapping
as he slips.

Creepy hotel

Creepy hotel,
northern town.
During daylight hours
it all seems normal
but after night-time falls,
it doesn't make
any sense to all.
Down one flight of stairs,
up three more,
maze like corridors.
Where is my door?

Creepy hotel
near the Yorkshire moors.
Walking down
twisting corridors,
like slipping through
a seeping
mist of slime.
You turn a corner
and face
the same corridor,
you've walked
a thousand times before.
Grotesque moans
echo through the bones
of these old rooms,
doorways like gravestones,
marking the place
of old ruins.

Creepy hotel.
In the dead of night.
Outside the banshees' howl,
loud enough
to give the devil a fright
and I am still traipsing
the same hallways,
the rickety staircase.
The creak it makes
when your foot dares
to touch its carpeted face.
The thud of my heartbeat
and the whistle of panting breath,
form an orchestra with the
creeping sound of death

Creepy hotel,
I've been walking for hours.
The same passageways,
the same endless towers.
By day it seemed
mere seconds away,
but at night
the ghostly architects
have been out to play.
I sway,
on the aching balls of my feet,
as the lingering fear chills my blood
and into bones it seeps.
I reach a door, turn the handle
and I spy myself asleep on the bed

As I am dragged back
into the corridors of the dead.

Angels guiding

I hear the distant song,
are the angels calling?
I feel I'm falling.
I may need their light,
are they going to sing?
I'm scared of this darkening night.

Are the angels watching?
Are they laughing?
At my misguided attempts
at being human
or are they sighing?
I can't see the wall for all the writing.
I don't know
how much more I can withstand.
I bury myself in sand,
not just my head.
I'm down deep
wishing I was dead.

Are the angels guiding?
Then I may have taken a wrong pathway.
Did they notice I was lagging?
That I was not smiling,
as much as grimacing,
whilst the day was flagging.
I don't know how much I can take,
my mind started to break
a long while back.
I'm under constant attack
from my own feelings.
My failings.
You may question my ways,
I question myself every day.

Are the angels guiding?
Or are demons hiding?
Riding forked lightning,
whist they stick out forked tongues.
I don't know if I can bounce back.
I've been flat for too long,
not a ball, nor a bat.
I'm just a person that tried
to find his cracked feet,
amongst the crazy paving
of these broken streets.

Are the angels guiding?
Or is the song in my head?
Repeating over and over again,
until my sense has fizzled out.
It's too much I shout
but the sky doesn't listen.
Though sometimes
tears of rain glisten,
when the sun comes out.

Are the angels calling me?
I may be a boat
adrift on stormy seas,
but I'm not ready
to hear their song.
I'll keep floating along.
Fingers in ears
because the song
has many verses
to be sung
and I want
a few more years.

False hope

All she was,
was false.
A deceiver.
A wolf
in sheep's clothing.
Draped in sin.
Dressed in fake bling
but with a flash
of that wicked grin,
she drew them all in.

Led them down
the garden path.
All she had to do
was fake a smile
Get them to splash
their hard-earned cash.
Then she would run a mile.

She knew what
she wanted
and how to get it.
Men were
easy to trick.
They only ever think with their...
Quick she thought
I've got the dough
now I just need to
get out of town
away we go.

Hope was fleeting.
Fleeing.
She had the spoils.
Her heart
was beating,
pacing,
pounding,
racing.
She left
in the time
it took
to hear
the sirens
gaining.

Eyes of moonlight

Eyes of moonlight
turn their sights on me.
I stand. Alone, afraid.
Of what?
I thought
as the stray sound
echoed in my head.
That lonely voice.
It whispered.

"What if the pain starts again,
what if the heavy rains fall on us today.
Why not just sit at home and hide away.
You know you can do this,
it's easier to just sleep into another day"

The lips of twilight
speak to me
in soft tones.

"Why do you stand alone?"

I try to speak,
the crackling sound
of a meagre voice,
straining to be unleashed,
to be more than just a scratchy noise.

"I struggle to be. Me.
I struggle to be understood."

Then the words come out in a flood.
In my head at least,
in reality,
barely audible squeaks.

The ears of the dusk light
hear my words,
they speak their night-time insights,

"Don't fear the outside world,
don't fear ridicule,
or possibly looking a fool.
Your voice is there,
It's just fear that stops
you from opening the door.
Let the light of midnight pour
over you and let yourself sway
to the music of the stars.
You have gotten this far."

The eyes of moonlight look upon me again,
shining, they speak dazzling words,

"Don't fear pain,
if it means a life not living.
Don't fear heartache,
if it means you can't share your love.
Don't fear life,
it's there for the taking,
Enjoy each minute,
before the reaper awakens"

HellHeaven

Maybe this is hell.
Screaming
into the void
every single day.
Feeling annoyed
at bleeding,
paper-cut hands,
that grip tightly
around my neck.
My own hands.
The internal conflict.

Maybe this is hell.
The words I speak,
creak
in withered agony
from torn,
ripped throat.
Worn and soaked
in salt water.
Stinging.
Screaming
not singing.

Maybe this is hell.
Locked in my shell,
a mental prison cell,
where no one hears
the screeching wails.
No one feels
the pulled nails,
the wind no longer
in my sails.

Or maybe
this is heaven.
The things we take for granted,
the beauty enchanted.
The wonder
that makes us ponder,
and contemplate everything.
The birds that sing,
the joy
that life can bring.
The love that comes
when you are
walking
that wobbly tightrope
and are all out of hope.

Feel

I feel her,
just behind.
Breathing
down my neck.
Hairs on end.
Goosebumps.
A shivering wreck.
I hear her
whispering
words of hurt,
seething
vicious worms
that climb
into your head.
They slither around
making you wish
that you were dead.

I feel her,
just behind.
I turn to look,
but she moves in time.
like a fading mist.
She flows,
just a second
out of my glance
but I know
she is there
trying to entrance.

I feel her,
just behind.
Her hands fixed
around my throat.
Tightly gripping,
fingernails ripping,
tearing,
I choke.
I can't reply.
I can't fight.
Just trapped
in her vice-like grasp.
A venomous snake,
her jaws around me.
Clasped.

I feel her,
just behind.
Fingers as sharp as knives,
cold as ice,
piercing my heart,
right through my spine.
I feel her,
Inside.
Ripping apart
all that has
been left behind.

Out of time

There are some fates
worse than that
of standing at hells gates.
Some fates worse than death.
That last breath.
Sometimes you come back.

Now don't get me wrong,
I didn't exactly long
to be gone,
or to be stuck in hell for eternity
nor heaven for that matter.
I was enjoying life,
alas that glass did shatter
and times fine sands scatter.

Time plays tricks with your mind.
I was remembering 1854,
the Crimean war had just begun,
I was supposed to be
fighting for queen and country
but then something happened to me.
I can't remember clearly.

I awoke in 1984 with puncture marks
upon my throat, an aversion to garlic
and a completely new distrust
of holy relics or symbols.
Sunlight burnt; I slept as others woke.
I walked the night-time streets.
Trying to make sense of a world
I didn't belong in, I was hungry.
The pain stung somewhere dark inside.
It sang to me in colours red and deep,
I needed blood to seep.
to help me find my peace.

I stalked the streets,
prowling the alleys.
The nocturnal city valleys,
the giant metal buildings frighten me.
Lights shone bright,
not gaslight,
some future magic.
I only know
I don't feel I belong,
I don't feel right.
I'm a man
out of time,
and the shadows
are my only lifeline.

Cravings

You had something
I was craving for,
I lusted after that juicy flesh
in between your
ears.
Your brain my dear.
For you see,
I'm a zombie.
A zed, one of the walking dead,
not like those rage filled guys.
I'm more Shawn of the dead
than 28 days later.
I just shuffle along,
not a new trend setter,
nor in any haste,
I just want brains.
I like the way they taste.

But I love to get my teeth
into some moist,
succulent brains.
I was surprised
I'll admit
and at first
it's hard to find
the right etiquette.
It all made me feel
a bit sick,
but once you've
acquired the taste
you would never
try a different dinner.
Though McDonalds
do seem
shockingly similar.

It makes people a bit
squeamish, nauseous,
to see us eat. I've tried to be polite.
No one wants grey matter
splattering their dinner plate.
I wear a bib,
bring a knife and fork with me.
I've even taken to cooking mine first.
Brains taste so much better that way.

I amble and stumble
most of the time,
I don't have to be anywhere,
there isn't much call
for zombies in the workforce.
To be fair, there isn't much call
for zombies at all.
Though I'm sure the Tories
are trying to find a purpose for us,
just to get us off benefits of course.

It isn't so bad,
hanging with the crew.
The conversation is dull
but no one else judges you.
We just shuffle through
the streets and towns.
Across the hills, over the downs.
We will see you soon I'm sure,
as you claw at your front door,
trying to escape the dreaded roar
of this zombie wave.
Searching in vain
to find any brains that remain,
in this backwater stain
on the universal plain.

A place called nowhere

A land where grim fairy tales
and nightmares hail you in,
smoke and mirrors shimmer,
leading to a place called nowhere.
Where rainbow lights
glisten and glimmer
like a twisted funfair
but don't be fooled
by the bright lights
or the colourful sights.
This is a land of darkness,
where vicious beasts
lurk in the night.

Staircases lead off
in all directions,
physically impossible
to navigate.
Surrounded by
vast empty holes,
where no light
can escape.
A waterfall of bright red,
flows up the walls,
like the room is spinning,
and blood is dripping.
Sudden growls echo
from the cavernous bowels below.

Through one doorway
a library,
aisles go on
for miles at a time,
over the horizon they dip.
Bookcases become doorways
at the touch of a spine.

They blur and shift
as the facade slips.
This palace of smoke and mirrors
never becomes any clearer,
like a world built of errors,
a maze of mistakes and
twisted grim heartaches.
In the distance
the howls
are getting louder.
Closer.
Heavier.
Prouder.

Time flows slower,
Sometimes it stops completely,
or reverses, like a tape
being rewound back to the start.
In this grim fairy-tale land,
you'll fear for your heart.
Where nightmares stand
in front of your eyes
and scream.
The tortured scream of so many bad dreams.
Skin from their faces dripping,
as they rip apart what remains,
leaving only the skeleton beneath,
and some maggot infested brains.
They keep you on your toes,
as you try to outrun,
always running,
never able to stop.
In this place called nowhere,
If you fall or stumble
it's your head for the chop.

Answers

I was looking for answers
and the world fell dark.
The sun clouded over.
Nothing, not a spark.
Just a void, where once
the universe sat.
The stars, once bright,
soon dimmed then clicked off.
No light.
No clear vision in sight.
I was looking for answers
but the universe
had other plans.

I was looking
and the words
became blurred.
Worlds shifted
out of focus,
I was lost deep
in greyscale dreams.
No colour held
within my field of view.
No rain.
No morning dew.
Just a blurred image
of nothing.
A vision
of a nightmare
coming true

Quiet reflection
in the rivers of life,
the mirrored sheen.
The tides stopped flowing,
nothing was showing.
I was looking for answers
and the skies fell silent.
I was looking
for answers
and nothing.

Is this oblivion
staring into me?

I wonder what it is it sees.

I was looking for answers
but I never had the questions it seems.

My shadow

As I walk under flickering streetlight,
the shadow I cast tries to escape.
Darting and dancing
but forever tied to me feet.
Follows every step I take.
It has seen my every high
and each stupid mistake

As I walk, he keeps the pace
If I try to run,
he gives chase.
Always right beside me,
it's as if we two, are one.
My shadow loves the sun
but when it's stormy
he jitters when the lightning comes

My shadow sees the lightness,
whilst holding darkness within.
He never gives me stress.
Even when my patience wears thin.
He just walks besides,
keeping stride, providing me company.
My shadow won't break away suddenly,
try to flee or leave me reluctantly.

And under those streetlights
he stands beside me close,
when I'm fearful of the night
and it's hoard of angry ghosts,
my shadow keeps an eye open,
even when mine are closed.
He blends in with the darkness,
Keeping those demons on their toes.

Hounded

I've heard him howl
through my own tears.
When I hear the screaming in my ears,
I've felt him near.
Growling, sensing the fear,
ready to pounce.
Always just a step behind.
Waiting for the moment
I lose my mind
and I scream to the sky.
Won't you clear this pollution from my eyes,
the grit covered cornea just brings sighs.

I've watched as he walks.
Just a few steps away,
I've seen his jaws, full of menace,
canines bloodstained
and rotting with decay
but he walks after me,
hunter to my prey.
So, I shout and pray,
Will anyone listen to what I say
but the words just fade
and desert me again today.

And that Big black dog
keeps following me home
Walking in my shadow,
Doesn't matter how far away I roam,
he always seems just a step behind me.
Chasing my skin covered bones.
And I say Lord. Will you spare me.
But he doesn't listen to my pleas.
So, I walk on regardless.
Through the ever-darkening trees.

TWO

**Though the path may be grim,
bones and rotten flesh
digging into the soles of our feet.
The path only leads
to the final destination
and the true horrors we meet.**

A cup of tea in Hell

The eternal howls
of the damned
are relayed over tannoy.
A torturous chorus of pain,
pumped through just to annoy.
As we wait...
Eternity.
Spent standing
in this piercing lava rain.
But hell isn't meant to be
a stroll in the park.

I took a wrong turning
somewhere up there,
I entered the wrong tunnel
like being in a crowded subway,
where disinterested commuters funnel.
It's sometimes hard to get your bearings,
the right train for where you are heading.
I must have picked the wrong platform,
Just following the herd trying to conform.
The fire and brimstone
should have been a sign,
a great big neon light
highlighting that my destination
was on the wrong line,
but my head
has always been in the clouds.
So, I just kept walking
along with the crowds.

I shouldn't be here,
but here I find myself
and I'm finding all new
facets to who I am.
New pieces of the jigsaw,
where no pieces fit before.
So, whilst I'm here
I may as well
make myself at home.

Demons watch
every little move you make,
a police state,
under constant surveillance,
navigating the 24 hour
cctv camera maze,
It's like home, only warmer.

Endless queues
as far as the eye can see,
insipid sips of stale warm tea.
Bits of broken biscuit floating
on its surface like a dingy on the sea.
Not so different
to dear old blighty.
Just some of the clientele
are a little more frightening.

Dreams & nightmares

Turn the handle and pull,
open the doorway full,
into the realm of dreams
and fantasy
as your visions
become a twisted reality.

Be they fleeting memories
of brighter days
or adventures
filled with mystery.
Enter the ethereal misty sea
of images.
Turn the pages
of the storybook world you inhabit.
For this is a good day,
a good night,
not fearful
or full of fright.

How soon it can change.
Dark clouds pour
angry outbursts of rain.
An outrage of horrors to explore,
as the dream swirls into nightmare
and the page flicks forwards once more.
Into the vast worlds of nowhere,
from fairy-tale to suspense.
The melting clock face
ticks backwards.
Chimes
booming and intense.

Hear the sounds
of your heart drumming,
as through warped corridors
you are running.
Floor sticky,
blood dripping
from the walls.
Pictures and paintings watch
as you stumble and fall.
Anxiety heightens,
your reflection, seen through foggy eyes,
shaking and frightened.
See through, transparent lies
stare back through the mirror void.
Reflective thoughts,
feeling paranoid.

Through the centre of the room
trees grow, a forest overgrown,
the trees themselves moan.
The sky in full view, no roof.
Two looming full moons
like eyes looking
down on you.
Lightning strike
paints a mouth
as the sky splits in two
and it slowly
bites down on you.

One hell of an open mic

Every word of this is true
or so I'm led to believe.
A poetry show,
one cold winters eve.
The words were flowing well,
the drink helped. But that wasn't a hard sell.
A buzz filled the hall
like insects wanted to join the thrall.

The host was making the guests feel inspired
like inside them they had burning, raging fires
and the words began to pop.
Twisting from lips, they wouldn't stop.
They bounced around the room into ears.
These words trapped away for years.
Finally freed.
Then something not normally seen in this poetry game,
the flow of words
started to erupt into flame.

Seems by twisting words
a little too well,
someone had accidentally
cast some mystic spell.
A direct line call to the gates of hell
and the Devil appeared, a bit dishevelled
and confused.
He was at that moment
just about to watch some TV.
His greatest creation.
Love Island.

Well, not one to turn down a free drink
and some entertainment.
The devil pulled up chair.
Which burned away instantly.
So, he stood listening intently
and he found the words flow through him,
a tear boiling in his fiery eyes,
a laugh roared
from his scorched throat
and in that moment, he swore
never to search for fiddlers again.
Poetry was may more hardcore.

It is said,
that on poetry nights,
if you look into the spaces
just out of the light.
You may see
his red fingers clicking,
hear
the fiery laughter ringing,
a smell of smoke.
So let you words out,
but be in no doubt
that sometimes the devil is lurking about

The walk of lost hope

Down the long dirt track,
cold metal barrel pressed against back.
The sound of shovel dragging,
snagging against roots
every few feet.
Could he escape?
Beat a retreat.

Down the long dirt track,
stretching limbs of rustling trees
grabbing him in the breeze.
He is pushed to his knees.
The shovel thrown in front.
Dig. The woman taunts.
Metal against dirt.

Sweat cascades from his forehead
like waves down a cliffside.
Nowhere to run.
Nowhere to hide.
3 foot deep now
and the moon sits behind a cloud.
Knowing what comes next.
If she had hands
she would cover her ears
from the fear, from the screams.
The bang splits the night in two.
the silence seeps out, red in hue.

The woman fills the pit,
dirt and grit
beneath fingernails.
She sits
smokes a cigarette and smiles
then walks away.
Hope was her name.

The hum grows

It's been too quiet
but now the hum is back,
louder than ever.
An aural attack.
It's crushing and pounding
every inch of my head.
The piercing screeching
of the restless undead.

It's been too quiet.
I should have known,
the peace was just a smokescreen
and now it's cover has been blown.
It's out in full force,
The noise. An unearthly voice
like violence
in auditory form.
Smashing through the silence,
breaching the calm.

It was too quiet.
I got complacent,
now my ears are bleeding
as is my nasal.
I feel it crushing the insides of my head.
Squeezing and squashing
it wants me dead.
It wants to force
all good from inside.
Drown it out with
its insidious grind.
I can't let it win
this monstrous din.
I drown it out with sounds,
music that pushes it
shaking to the ground.

Deja vu

Been here before,
I can remember this scene
like I was walking here one day
sometime in a stolen dream

I remember the faces,
the way I sense movement,
it's like I'm not in control.
Pulse in my neck races.
through automated eyes I stare,
my gaze not mine.
It feels I'm being pulled
in one direction. I can't turn my head.
I can't explain. Nor unwire my brain
to look the other way instead.

Been here before,
can remember the scene.
I have lived this moment
in cycles it seems.
I go with the flow.
No choice. It's their show.
My eyes only look where they are told,
limbs only move where
memories tell me to go.
I see a note written in red ink.
Blood? It says, *"turn your head."*

But why do they always lead back here?
Is it this place I seek?
This door. This hand grabbing the handle.
Mine. It feels disembodied.
The door inches open with a grinding creak.
Sounds like the gates to hellish eternal penitentiaries,
feels like a tomb that hasn't been entered in centuries.

In the darkness, a hand beckons me in.
A cackled laugh.
I can picture a toothless grin.
As the creature within leaps
for my exposed throat.
I keep going back
to the note.
Turn my head.
I look to my side.
There is a knife, almost within my grasp.
In the blood that pours from my ripped torn throat
I scrawl myself a note.
One day I may be able to break the cycle.
It's my only hope.
Darkness cloaks...

Been here before,
I can remember this scene
like I was walking here one day
sometime in a stolen dream...

Forever in shade

Forever left in shade,
under the aching tree,
as it watches.
Mournfully
over me.
Branches reach out,
but never quite touch.

Falling leaves
coating my skin,
like earth being thrown
upon the heavy lid
of my coffin.

Forever is delayed,
being led away,
a different path to me.
Led astray
with dreams
dancing
into tomorrow's
fading yesterdays.

Sometimes dreams
are meant
to be broken.
Shattered and scattered,
to the wind like dust.
Forever is delayed
and time is almost up.

Forever left in tears.
It never seems
to stop raining in here.
A constant downpour.
Can the sun reach out
to where I beckon?
Dry these tears
that are getting leaden.
So that I can see clearly.
if only for a second.

Or will I be
forever left
upon this shelf
of broken hearts,
always trying
to rebuild myself.

Kyle Coare

I hear them

I hear them
clawing,
scratching and pawing
at my bolted doorway.
The rattling sound,
clicking and cracking,
skittering flurries,
hurried and scurried.
Slithering sounds
join the thrum,
an aural maelstrom.
All trying to get in.
"What do they want from me"
I think.

I hear them,
as they screech
against the windowpane,
like nails down a chalkboard.
An assault on the brain.
Cold ice flows
through my
terror filled veins.
"Wont they leave me be"
the words spill,
shivering as if
I've caught a chill.

I hear them on the rooftop
like stormy raindrops,
then they stop.
Silence. Nothingness.
I hear just my breathing.
Air fighting to fill my lungs.
Wheezing, and my hearts drumbeat
like the firing of a hundred guns.

They are inside,
nowhere I can hide.
I see shapes in the gloom.
Jittery spider-like creatures in my room.
I see others, reptilian and slimy,
I dive for my covers
as they slither beside me.
Sliding, writhing on empty bellies,
ready to feast on me.

Child sized centipedes
with eyes that bleed.
Spiders with a dog's growl,
dripping poison from their jowls.
Fangs as sharp as a butcher's knife,
wanting to put an end to my life.
Snake-like creatures fill the spaces,
my heart races, feeling feint.
My vision fades.

I wake with a start. In my room.
I check my limbs.
Intact.
I check my heart. Still beating.
Sunlight peering through the curtains.
In the corner of my eye
I spy a shadow creeping by,
and I hear a sound
that makes me want to cry.
I hear them scratching and clawing,
slithering and pawing,
as the sun goes dark.
My windows covered
in the spiders that bark.

In too deep

In too deep.
Sheltered
from the rain,
but drowning
in the muddy ground
left behind.

I never knew darkness
could come in shades
as deep as these.
I never believed that
the cold
could consume me,
I never perceived my grave
as this dark place,
just a bed of thorns to pierce,
thinking I'd be brave.
I never knew that pain
could be so fierce
and just like that,
I collapsed out of the fight.

I never knew I could cry
knives instead of tears
but I knew I could
come back stronger
and my wings still fly.
I poured my heart,
I poured the hurt,
I poured my rage
into words staining
the tear-soaked page.

I never knew
that hearts were
so fragile,
made to be broken
along this bumpy trial.
I never knew.
that I'd hold death
so close.
I never knew
he would follow me
everywhere I go.
That my feelings
would be stolen.
But I knew that
I'd get through.
Cursed though I am
to spend so long
in my own shadow.
Watching
as it swallowed
me whole.
I knew I'd break out,
punch through
I just had to put
one foot in front
of the other
and walk
towards you.

Kyle Coare

Ghost stories

There have been countless
ghost stories worldwide
What is it that fascinates us so,
about passing over to the other side?
Is it facing our greatest foe?
Time.

Is it the thought that we can cling on tight
Even when we should be entering the light,
that a part of us can still survive
or is it fear of a life lived,
not truly alive.

When our story closes
a slammed book
like a coffin lid
hammered shut,
when our sands trickle
to the other end of the glass
and we realise
that what we have had
has passed.

There have been countless
romance tales told,
so intrinsically linked
in golden ink.

And the story...
Love and death
arms joined in eternal glory.
Ghosts that don't realise they've died.
Hearts that are bound and tethered
unable to cross to the other side.

There is romance in the fiction
haunting memories
that live on
in those stories
of grey ladies
walking aimlessly
across the balustrades,
to look out once more,
for just a sign
of lovers who never return
but whose memories burn
eternally into the mists of time.

Late

Tick tock, tick tock.
Suddenly it stops.
It's 4 am again
or so the clock beside me states.
All I know is its late.

Silence. Deathly silence.
Stalks around the room,
stealthily it fills the air
like cotton wool placed deep in the ear.
Absorbing every sound.
Dissolving each noise before it starts.
Dulls every thumping beat of the heart,
every pounding thud. Now just a vibration.
Feels like a million miles from here.

Darkness, the creeping darkness.
Hides the monsters that lurk amongst us.
Now my room is the place it resides.
From the darkness, there is nowhere to hide.
You can feel it clinging close to your skin,
icy brushes wear your patience thin
like damp clothing dripping. Chilling.

Time, the slow seconds,
bestowing fear.
Time never seems to move
when you are stuck here.
Trapped in this glacial nightmare groove
when the record keeps repeating the same refrain.
Over and over again.
4 am the clock still states.
How can that be. Time smiles in wait.

Alone. I know I'm not alone.
but I know no-one is home.
I know that no one living
is present in my room.
but I feel,
I fear
hands come near.
I fear,
the feel of fingers
touching my hair.
Startled.
I try to scream.
The whimpering
is all that comes
as the clock slowly ticks once more.
I sink into
another nightmare dream.

Ink

Something out there
is pulling us in.
My head is saying run.
Legs are just following
the pathway into the beyond,
where the thick raven darkness
dominates the view
like a solid brick wall,
no features,
no shades of colour,
no subtle markings
just a wall of nothing
and that's right where
our feet are going.

We cling tight as the
liquid gloom
coats our skin.
We hold each other
in embrace,
as the darkness tastes
our sin.
In this fearful place,
the dark,
a living breathing thing.
We hold tight,
walking closely
through the charcoal sight
as thick as night,
the inky black ensures fright

Halfway through,
I feel fingers gripping
onto my shoes,
I feel brushes
as hands reach out to touch us
but I see nothing.
Just the jet-black void.
Each step could be the last
but we can't turn back.

I hear breathing,
hearts beating,
then realise they're ours,
echoing loud.
I hear the others.
Their whispers, the slurp of licked lips.
I focus on the heart beats
and pray that the end will be quick.
I hold your hand.

Then the murkiness collapses around us,
we are back where we started.
Sun light beams down,
birds sing,
and for a second I think
I'll never let the darkness win,
life is too beautiful a thing.

Blanket of night

Moonlight casts
her shadows,
far and wide.
Bountiful places
to play and hide.
Open spaces to lay
and watch the sky tonight.
To watch the stars
in fascinating dancing flight
like candles burning
through the blanket of night.

The moon sees all,
hears our cries.
Every dropped call,
every exalted high.
She sees the watchman
standing at his door,
as the rains pour
only around him,
a constant downpour.

She has seen
oceans boil,
welcoming life,
seen it take
its first strides
on the soil.
She saw the
dinosaurs munching grass,
carnivores
hunting the weak,
she saw the comet crash
and a world whose
future looked bleak.

She will be here
long after we are gone.
She knows the evils that lurk.
She has watched in terror
the horrors
of humans at work.
She sees every misdeed,
every hand of greed
stealing food
from those that need to feed.

She sees the hate,
the weight
around her neck
is tight.
She cries
every night.
but then sees
some beauty in life
and her smile grows,
big and wide.

Snaps

I can feel the dissonance,
the harmonious nature of everything
has stopped singing.
I can hear the final bells
of the universe ringing.
It's all distorted,
the world feels off centre
like the gates of hell have opened
and the demons have started to enter.

Disparity in the way the air moves,
no more clarity to the view,
it's all contorted and disjointed.
Deranged landscapes are twisted
like the poles have shifted
before my eyes.
Items appear from thin air,
yesterday they were not there.

I feel the world is out of order,
I can sense the discordance,
the universal shifting borders.
Things you can't explain,
nothing rational remains.
Unexplainable
when the rain flows the wrong way
but you know that this
isn't the work of a tired brain.

Can feel the clash of reality
and the so-called imaginary.
Disconnected from the way
life should be.
When you see things,
where they shouldn't be seen.
When visions appear
then vanish just as quick
as the first pangs of fear
start to prickle your skin.

You know in your heart
that everything
is as it should be,
or that's what your mind
is selling you.
But the way the world
is upside down,
is telling a completely different truth.
Because something inexplicable
is seeping in through the cracks,
the ones that are left
when the universe snaps.

Stage

This stage used to be her playground,
when the crowds would come in droves,
her name always top of the bill.
In flowing Victorian clothes,
she always stole the show.
This stage, under the spotlight,
she would wow and delight
night after night.
In this theatre stage show city,
where things seem
so bright and pretty
but in the darkness
the slime sticks
and the air is gritty.

The stage used to be
her playground,
but to get there
she spent so much time
laying down.
So much time
giving favour to repugnant suits,
who thought she was their slave,
to do as they wished.
"Never speak of this with your lips.
Never speak or we will make
you wish you were down in the pits."
They would hiss, in serpentine call.
She never wanted any of this,
just to be adored is all.
To perform
for an audience,
to feel the applause
ripple through her bones,
her skin, to feel the joy
of the people as she would sing.

This stage used to be
her playground,
where the sounds
would reverberate around,
the voices booming,
the songs longingly soothing,
but there was always malice looming.
And one eve it did come,
she turned down the wrong man,
and down a trapdoor,
into the darkness,
under the stage,
her blood did run.

Now she watches
from the shadows.
You will see her if you look close,
her face haggard
and broken down.
Her Victorian gown
outdated and torn.
Translucent she floats through.
Once more teary eyes
take to the stage.
Her yells, her cries
still echo in the darkness
as she tries to tell
the young girls to flee,
scaring them
to make them leave
with their lives.

Kyle Coare

Phantom words

There are ghosts
in the words.
Haunting moans sit
anticipating their release,
like delicate wisps of smoke
tingling on cold lips.
I feel them
pulling away from my grip,
slip into the air and float there.
Aimless and free.
Phantoms roaming
between you and me

There are ghosts in the verses.
Dead to us,
apparitions of hope,
see through nooses,
transparent old rope.
To remind of places
where our memories elope.
I could follow where
those sombre words flow
but then all I'd find
is a dried riverbed
where roses
can no longer grow.

There are ghosts
in the things we say.
Spirits speak
in echoes of yesterday.
Spectres of truth float lifelessly
on the still lying sea,
where honesty is drowned
under the surface, in agony.

There are ghosts
in the words.
Devilish melody of
maladies and bad chemistry,
poison-tinged remarks
and snarky acid sprayed barks.
Spoken in spluttered bursts,
the words seem cursed.
Could whisper through the fear
but that could bring so much pain,
so instead, I pull the words back
and store them, locked up,
in my fearful brain.

Well

That circle of light
like the moon up above.
Remembering
what you thought of as love.
It all came crashing,
rushing through your mind
Now the memories are so hard to find.

The slow echoing drip,
cold hands that grip.
Seeping into your skin.
Sleeping and weeping,
caked-in years of dirt and grime
in this hole with no time.

The walls, slimy and damp.
The light of the moon
in these confines so cramped.
The ache of your neck,
twisted and cracked.
The small of your back,
broken on impact.

Drip. Drip. Drip.
The slow passage of time
like the waters that fill this tomb
dripping slowly past you.
It's cold.
So cold.
Bones old, broken
body crumpled
in a way it isn't meant to fold.

That circle of light,
so far up above,
not the moon,
but the place from which
you were shoved.
Where you breathed
your last breath.
This well
that is filled
with the rancid
stench of death.

Kyle Coare

On the wisp of the wind

On the wisp of the wind.
I hear your voice,
chilling me to the bone.
In every drop of rain
I hear your gurgled moan,
the rattle of chains,
the thunder outside
and the screams
over and over again.

Gone for so long
but somehow still you are there.
It's like you surround me
I feel your presence in the air.
Every footstep I take,
I hear a second in reply
and that strangled cry
follows me,
probably will until the day I die.

A cold hand of fear holds me there,
in the air I hear the groans and despair.
Trickling down my spine,
I feel fingers frigid and icy.
I see visions of you looking at me
and that look on your face,
wretched and torn,
lost and forlorn.
The gaping mouth
screaming for help,
when help is long gone.
I see dead eyes
staring into oblivion,
only replaying the misery,
reflecting the images that I see.

On the wisp of the wind,
on its waves your words sail.
They rise and fall
with each tidal exhale.
I feel them
trying to drag me under
like a tentacled beast
from below the blue wonder.
I feel the groans
start to infiltrate my mind.
I hear the drone
of the anger that resides.
I fear that soon
I'll be nothing but these tones,
when they have drowned out
the sounds of my own.

Remembrance

She stands.
this lady in grey.
A faded view
on a foggy day.
She waits
beside
these
cemetery gates.
She stands
head in her hands.
Her longing tears
concealed
by slate coloured veil.
Lonesome heart
sealed
in a vault
of ice-cold steel

She walks through
the gravestone city.
Her feet
never in view,
never leaving a footprint
in the cold autumn dew.
Just fades
between the stones.
Lost and alone.
Look of concern arises.
Swirling storm filled skies
fill the irises
of her grey eyes

She stands
at the tomb entrance.
Her eyes entranced
by the name etched
on the marble plaque.
Her name sits staring back.
Remembrance.
She sinks into the walls,
through the floor
and down
to her place of rest.
Her eyes filled
A steady rain.
phantom tears,
as they close again.

Empty, endless streets

Empty endless streets
I shuffle through,
like they are on repeat.
Keep eyes
to the ground,
only staring
at the scruffy shoes
on my feet.
For if I lift my gaze
and look around,
I'll be scared
of the sight I'll meet.

Was so different
before the bombs came,
before the fallout rain
swamped the ground
in its fiery pain.
There used to be
life around,
sounds abounding
from the shops and buildings.

Replaced with deathly silence
on these empty endless streets.
Now I just dream
of those old days,
before the blast
of neutron rays,
before the decay and agony.
before the bad winds
blew it all away.

The crumbling old cinema
used to show movies all day,
so many stories contained within its shell.
So many stolen kisses, lost glances,
now all that dances
are the fallout particles
and embers on the wind.
Now it just resembles hell.
Scorched, broken walls,
old paint blisters.
How I miss the old life.
How different it would be
if the rockets had missed us.

Supermarket shelves
ransacked and ravaged,
the life that remained
fought to scavenge.
The old tins and produce
Now all gone, only so much food
to go around.
Others went to ground.
They never returned,
It's just me now and this lonely
old war-torn town.

Past the old school block,
in the old days this would be alive,
children running and playing.
Now echoes of long dead memories
no longer thrive.
Down my old road,
born and raised in this abode,
it now just sits
derelict, broken to bits
Just a reminder of the missile hits.

Listen

Listen to the car crash symphony,
a heart-breaking melody of melancholy
inside my head.
No sympathy.
Just cataclysmic crashing cymbals and dread.
When you can't see a way forward
just satanic symbols leading you astray.
Betrayal and pain follow
in every whispered word they say.
The path behind swallowed up.
There is no silver lining
to life's brittle China cup.

Listen to the sound
of a world crashing all around
like waves of destruction,
towers being pulled down,
replaced by statues,
everything you despised.
Statues of lies
built up in front of your eyes.
High Rise, they pierce the sky
until tears of blood are cried.

Listen to my own internal monologue
like a travelog,
taking me to distant torture spots.
A life-sized cardboard cut-out image,
just there to look like I'm there,
when I'm in another location
and they are painfully pulling
out my nasal hair.
One by one. With tweezers.
Demons
with angelic features.

Listen to the silence
as my mind finally collapses,
just the sound of static
buzzing quietly through
burnt out synapses.
As I fall into a dark pit.
To recharge for a bit.
Before recommencing the climb.
The climb to find my place in life,
to push aside this noise and strife,
to feel I have a place to belong.
It will take some time.
Who knows how long?

Kyle Coare

A single shot

A shot cuts the air,
spinning to its target
against the still cold of night
as the gunman lifts his eyes
from the barrel sight.
The world won't ever be the same,
a single shot
to ignite years of hurt and pain,
To light the fires
under the melting pot.

A single shot.

A single shot starts every war,
just one finger on a trigger,
pulled taught.
The sound rings out,
deafeningly loud,
piercing the peace before
an onslaught of noise
as all sides have the excuse
they were looking for

A single shot,
one lone bullet.
Forced into the air at such speed.
One finger on a trigger,
how different the world,
if he didn't pull it.
How many innocents wouldn't
have had to bleed
A single shot, one barked command.
An order, now the flames have been fanned.
One body down, no stopping.
The tinderbox is lit, the bodies
start dropping.

Inner voice

This nagging feeling
like an ever closening sea,
isn't inching
towards me,
it's rushing forward
like the ghostly woman
from the ring,
climbing out of her tv.

The intense feeling
to which I am resigned
like a drill bit
driving deep into my mind.
The wailing sound
it makes,
screeching in agony.
Is occupying every
bit of my head,
grinding my teeth,
until my mouth is all
blood and bone instead.

The wretched soundtrack
of my own internal voice,
giving negative feedback,
never applause.
It just screams and curses,
utters words of terse adversity.
It mutters that I'm not worth anything.
It shouts and spits.
Ripping my peace of mind to bits
and then it sits
happily watching me
crawling in the dirt,
collecting my shattered thoughts
and repairing the hurt.

Mental fog

Driving through mental fog,
can't see the road in front of me.
Could be heading
to a cliff edge
or a forest
full of trees.
Headlights approaching,
full beam
blinding already tired eyes,
distorting
distracting with visual lies.
I'm lost.
Hazard lights blinking,
thoughts no longer thinking.
Breakdown imminent.
So, I stop
and survey my predicament.

On foot I traipse
through the mental sludge,
each foot fall heavier
with this cerebral mud.
Flagging.
My aching bones,
muscles and joints,
mind ragged and torn,
can't figure which way
the compass points.
I want to stop,
lay down in this emotional slop
and let the world just spin,
whilst I fly off.

Further on I walk.
Heavy sodden footsteps,
internal talk.
Voices telling me to quit,
what's the point?
Stop and sit.
Let the ground swallow,
be buried in a grave,
swampy and shallow.
For there are some you can't save.
Brace the weather,
wait until forever
has been and gone
and admit
that the murkiness
has finally won.

Bewildering visions all I see,
silhouettes of crooked trees
reaching, grabbing out for me.
I'd run, but the ground
is tugging at my feet,
pulling me in,
a mortal morsal to eat.
So, I walk with fear,
my good old friend.
Hope this fog
will soon end
and the weather will clear,
maybe then
I'll find a pathway
out of here.

Locked

Shackled in place,
can't let go of doubt,
the feeling of low worth.
Can't be erased.
Can't break out.
Locked in a brain shaped box,
a prisoner of life.
Who can open the locks?
Untangle chains that bind.

Locked in mind,
self-hating brain,
behind walls built
to withstand pain,
tried to scramble clear
but the cell filled with fear
like deep waters rising
gasping, crying.
Thoughts flooded out
rivers of doubt.

The prisoner
of mind and heart,
a thinker torn apart.
Now locked in a new hell.
A shiny new cell.
Senses that won't depart
ripped feelings
scar his new start.
Soul lets out a scream,
from within
agonisingly deep
negative dream.

Locked down
in self-hate,
wants to feel
reborn,
open up
his prison gate,
throw down
the crown of thorns,
not slip on icy ground.
Stand tall
and proud
but the prison
of life
keeps grinding
him down.

Name the ghosts

I could name the ghosts.
I could speak of them.
I could but what good would come
from digging up old corpses?
So many,
stories.
Where the edges get distorted,
some of the facts misreported.
You are transported
back to a time you remember,
only the walls have been rebuilt.
The blueprints passed
in Chinese whispers,
So now the door sits,
where before sat
an old coffee table,
engraved with years of rings,
like a tree of caffeine addiction.

The nicotine yellow stains
cloud everything,
in sepia toned memory.
Faded in times' steady rains
and walking through
the wailing echoed strains
of a melancholic brain,
the shadows of old names.
Washed out ink
blotting the page.
faces that became dust
and blew away
on the wind.

I could name
the demons.
Every one of them.
I could talk of the hell
they led me to,
I could walk through
those corridors,
with my eyes closed tight
with superglue,
but really, what good would it do?
I've clawed myself clear,
I've ripped my eyelids apart,
so now I see everything,
not just the greying
yellow stains on my heart.

Lies

All lies,
Arise,
see the look in dead eyes,
doubts sown in voices
intoned with false highs.
All lies.
Some surprise
when you see so much,
yet your heart never flies,
always grounded,
happiness in short supply.

All lies.
Liars don't hide.
They paint themselves tall
with colourful signs,
pride themselves on how many fall
for their jagged lines.

The perfect crime,
a murder of trust.
Poisoning of hope,
a robbery of love.

All lies.
So, don't expect me to stand by
watching the sky fall
and tears stall.
I don't have the time
to become a victim of this hurt tonight.
I have too much stored in my pantry
in my mind sanctuary,
my shadowed hallway,
lined with boxed thoughts I threw away.
In my garden overgrowing.
In my kitchen the taps of pain are left flowing.

All rise.
To look
in the eyes
of those whose
lies
dampened
your sunrise.
Don't sigh.
Don't despise, don't despair.
Nothing is beyond repair.
Be wise.
Find eyes
that look back
with care
with arms wide open,
that want to share.

Demonic dance

From the foot of my bed,
I felt icy cold dread,
fingers pulling at sheets
and that voice.
The gurgled roar
of the undead,
sounds almost like
thunder crashing
through my head.

The smoky demons spoke
in grating tones.
Unintelligible,
rasping reverberating moans,
cut through with staccato shouts,
groans around sinister pouts.
They circled and flew about.
Always moving,
So, I was trapped throughout.

They glared with eyes of red,
fangs of yellow glinted like blades.
They bared their teeth,
in vicious snarls.
Growling,
Laughing. Howling gnarls.
The wicked words twisted
like branches
from an old, crooked bramble tree.
They were here to devour me.

Long past midnight,
they leapt about,
with such purpose and glee.
Manic, frightfully stuttering
in the strobing glare
of fluorescent light.
I panic. I want to flee
but there is no way through.

This grim dance like an impenetrable wall.
No cracks to break through,
nowhere to crawl.
I close my eyes.
Tight.
I let the demons win
as their icy fingers
touch my skin.

Kyle Coare

Ghostly patrol

Wind whistling,
whipping up a storm.
Ripping through the trees
and causing much alarm.
I'm inside,
where I should be calm...
But this house is haunted
and someone has
dropped the fear bomb.

This house is haunted,
I hear it creaking,
scratching
dragging chains,
what evil plan
is it hatching?
I'm wracking my brain.
It's picking up the pace,
clanking up the staircase.
then inside my room,
I lay, filled with dread.
Footsteps stop dead.
at the foot of my bed
and then the yelling starts.
Aimed directly at my head.
It screams. So loudly.
I fear the windows will shatter,
along with my brain,
as I picture the walls plastered
with my splattered grey matter.

This house is haunted.
I hear its cursed voice
coursing through the walls
like blood pumping
through veins.
My heartbeat stalls.
I hear terrifying incantations,
demonic aberrations.
I'm getting palpitations.
Vibrations rocking
the very foundations
and I'm struggling,
I'm gasping.
I'm gripping on tightly
and the vision
is now standing
right beside me.

This house is haunted
and I cannot move.
I'm tied to my bed,
my body weighed down
by my duvet of lead.
All I can do
is close my eyes
and imagine the sounds
are just the weather outside.
In this eternal night-time
of the lonely soul,
I'm stuck here
with this ghostly patrol.

Bus stop

Standing at the looming bus stop,
the sign hanging over me
like a guillotine about to drop.
Slowly dreading walking away
from what I was thinking.
Already starting
to miss the feeling.
Am I sinking?
I don't know
if leaving is right,
but I know I'd end up
regretting
staying the night.

You can't place a lid
on exposed thoughts,
they are out,
floating
caught in the urgent current
of the wind.
Trapping what remains,
and blending it in.
A lid
won't stop the rest
from flying away.
You can't stem the flow
or dam the pain,
where rivers of hurt
choose to go.
Returning to the scene
won't change
the way things used to be.
Won't transform the hurt
into happy memories.

A stone statue,
staring absently
into the gloom.
If I don't move soon,
I'll grow roots.
Here, the bus stop still looms,
watching my thoughts
rushing through.
I'm thinking in abstracts,
just to distract my mind
from memories of you.
The mind doesn't keep things simple,
it sometimes slips and tumbles a bit.
It never sits still when I want,
it just flows from thought
to unfinished thought.
Caught in the headlights
as the bus creeps in.
I start to see the light,
blinding with insight.
I realise,
I left
because
it wasn't
feeling right.
So, if you think
I'm on the edge of breaking,
I'm not so fragile. Though aching,
my heart is stitched up tight.
My soul has walked
through darkness
and strolled in light.
I'm not gonna fall.
My head is held high,
I step on the bus
and watch
as night has arrived.

Losing sleep

I seem to be losing sleep.
Don't know where I put it.
Maybe it's the bleary-eyed scrolling
through Facebook's rolling pages,
on twitter swiping down for ages.
Hours on messenger conversing,
Spotify listening
to my favourite musicians sing.
Instagram images flood through my head,
Reddit threads keep me awake in my bed.

I seem to be losing sleep,
I'm sure I had it before.
Maybe it is beneath the debris,
the remnants of me,
that carpet the floor.
I could have left it in the fridge,
I'd better check, I open the door.
Could be behind the day-old sandwich
or the coke bottle mountain,
the stale cheese, the cornish pasties.
hmm I'm getting peckish,
I'll cook up some supper while I'm at it.

I seem to be losing sleep,
I looked behind my eyelids
doesn't seem to be there,
just a bunch of sheep leaping around
and they really don't seem to care.
They just jump the fences.
disturbing the thoughts that I keep isolated.
Scattering them around
and no matter how late it is
they fill my head with their constant sound.

Arecibo

We sent out signals,
signpost sounds,
messages to the stars.
Telling them
where we are.
We gave them
our vital stats,
lots of facts,
at the speed of light.
Into the wilderness of space.

We gave details of our DNA,
the building blocks of life,
we told them how we survive.
In multiple frequencies,
every radio wave,
every TV broadcast,
every single transmission,
we poured our messages
to the stars.

And they heard. Every word.
They listened to the dictators.
Our political leaders.
They listened to our warlike cries,
saw the bloodlust in human eyes.
They saw as innocents died,
to provide profit to our darker sides.
They watched as people lied
and war-torn countries
smouldered under missile fire.
They watched.
They cried.
Then they turned back.
No stopping this human genocide.

When night falls the watchman calls

When night falls
the watchman calls

He strums his guitar to the aching wind,
soothing her gently, so that she will sing
and not scream.
For even the night does dream.
Even the weather
feels the agony and terror
of the beasts
that come together
on these cold, cold nights.

He patrols,
like a hunter in search of prey,
He can smell the rot and decay,
it lingers when the demons
have been at play.
He searches
high and low,
amongst the debris
of the guttural overflow.
No nook or cranny
does he overlook
When the night is dark,
and the demons have struck.

The air stills, then screams in pain.
She sees what will happen next
and she cries tears of rain.

In the dark moonlight,
On this cold harsh night,
the watchman walked into a trap.
The demons circled,
and ripped
the guitar
from his back.
Stamped their marks
over his face,
with boots of lead and hate.
The watchman was down,
His eyes drowning in the red
seeping from his head
as the night turned pitch black.

When the night calls
the watchman falls.

Last orders

Spirits soak into every pore,
slowly drip from the beer tap.
Stir up memories of older days,
as they drip softly to the floor.

Last orders the bell would ring.
Drink up the barmaid would sing.

Laughter still reverberates
when the place is empty,
cries and tears,
of which there have been plenty.
They all soak in.
Weathered into the wooden bar top,
like it's made of porous skin.

Spirits in every nook and cranny,
everywhere you look
a faded memory.
The highs and the lows.
This place has seen them all.

Every barstool a story,
every drunken stumble, every fall.

Each and every day,
open doors welcoming,
hidden hands making them sway,
beckoning in.
Home from home,
but in here
the phantoms roam.

Hidden from sight,
the spirits take over
when the place closes at night.
Pint glass pushed
by unseen hands
teeters towards the edge
then drops.

Smashes where it lands.

The scent of pipe smoke fills the air.
In the old coal fireplace
wispy flames
begin to flare.
Darts fly,
pool balls clunk together.
The arrows head
straight for the bullseye.
The sound of disembodied voices,
echoing a wartime cry.
Chatter and laughter,
smiles and sighs.
Anger and love,
emotions don't die,
they live on
in the brickwork
and they come out at night.

Red lights

I see the red lights,
red eyes?
In the distance glaring.
Staring?
Are they getting nearer?
Is my vision becoming clearer?
I hear my breath catching.
animals scratching?
Or…
The words don't want to come out.
Words don't want to play,
the words don't want to scream.
They are sat cowering in fear today,
circling like bad thoughts
down the drains of bad dreams.

I see the glistening shine,
Is it it moonlight on teeth?
Or just the reflection of light
from a dew dropped leaf.
For a second, fear subsides,
I laugh inside,
a stilted unsure chuckle,
as I still fear.
There is something near.
The sounds still scuttle.
I sense danger,
a feeling that troubles.
I want to get away quick,
apprehension doubles

I hear the sound,
shutters drop over eyes,
I hear the thud,
as my body crumples,
to the dirt and mud.
A hammer blow to the head.
I taste blood.
Dripping into the corners
of my mouth.
I see visions dance across
the corneas of my eyes.
I see…
The words don't want to say it.
They don't believe my eyes.
They pray it, is all just a trick of the light.
But I know it. The figure looming in the dark.
It is you.
And you just plunged
a knife
deep into my heart.

Curse

The moon was full,
I heard the howls.
Agonised screams,
heart-breaking cries.
A dark mist did fall,
walking through
ink-stained clouds.
I heard the growls.
The call of evil
from all around.

My heart raced,
beating through my chest
trying to escape
this dreaded test.
Ice cold fog clinging,
tightly sticking
to my skin.
A startling sound,
much bigger than a dog.
I could hear its paws
cracking bones
like twigs.

Pawing the ground.
Faster,
it began to pound.
Closer.
Closer.
It was getting near
but I only saw shadows
in misty fear.
Twisted illusions
in the fog filled air.

A roar echoed.
Loud
and so close,
I can almost smell its breath.
Sour
and full of death.
Then through the mist
a furry limb,
sharp claws
deeply slicing
into my goose-bumped skin.

And now it stands over me.
Tall and proud.
Howls at the moon,
buries his head
against my neck.
Hot breath.
Stomach sick.
A sound.
A loud crack in the night.
Gunshots pierce the air
The animal runs in fright

But forever I'll be
connected to him.
His pain flows freely
through my veins
and when the moon is full
I'll be out on the prowl,
it's my curse forever.
The wolf will howl.

THREE

THREE

**The shadows warned us,
but we didn't hear their cries.
The shadows warned us,
at the cold dark end of day.
The shadows warned us
and now the beast
is on his way.**

The stopped clock

Tick tock.
Tick.
Tock.
Ti...
The clock stopped.
Both hands held straight up
like surrendering to the night.
All around, silence gripped tight.
The calm before the storm.
A hint of malevolence,
then the air started to drip. Transformed
into a thick heavy slick
of oily black unpleasantness.
The air tasted rancid,
the scent of rotten flesh implanted
deep inside the nose
and with a pincer grip it stuck tight.

The air still,
no sounds,
no movement.
No wind brushed curtains
swaying against the windowsill.
Even the dust particles
were barricaded and still.
Startled, the moonlight faded.
it was like time had ceased,
become weak and fatigued,
a completely different beast.
It was empty and needed to feed.
The only thing that moved,
lived, breathed,
was me.
Time was ravenous you see,
I was the main course
and I had nowhere to flee.

I could feel time eating away,
tearing at my skin,
agonisingly ripping away the flesh
like hungry wolves around a fresh kill.
My life was devoured,
it quickly soured,
I could feel the passing of ages
in the aching of bones, weariness
behind my eyes, my thighs
couldn't hold my weight,
my legs buckled
and on the ground, I lay,
like a steak on a dinner plate.
Slowly being eaten away
by the unseen mouth of time.

I glanced around through fading eyes,
the mirror I spied.
I wanted to look away,
but my eyes wouldn't stray
from the reflection,
the face,
staring my way.
For it was not the one
I saw earlier in the day.
This one was older, wrinkled,
weary and grey.
The lights faded away.
Only the black void
and the sound drifting, softly upward.
The final sounds I heard.
ck.
Tick.
Tock.
Tick.
Tock.
Tick tock.

Kyle Coare

My life as a blood sucking beast of the night

I don't want immortality,
to see everybody I know
fall apart before me.
It's a curse that I was granted.
All I have to do
is avoid holy relics, stakes,
sunlight, blessed water, garlic flakes,
getting buried alive amongst the worms
with not even enough room to turn.
It's a wonder I have survived this long,
hundreds of years have been and gone,
since that cloaked figure pierced my neck.

If I'd just said no
when he wanted inviting in.
I would have just grown old in this skin.
But now it's all,
up at the crack of night,
flap about in the form of a bat
looking for a bite.
Creeping in shadows,
seeking my lunch,
a victim on which to munch.
I don't even like the taste of blood
like copper coins,
warm, It's really not so good.
How I'd kill for some French cuisine,
but garlic could be the death of me.

My lair,
a council flat in disrepair.
I'd call customer services
but the opening hours are a real hassle.
We don't all get allocated castles.
I'm not a count or anything,
though I do wear a cloak.
People think I'm eccentric,
they shout abuse
from their porches
I'll take it,
I'd rather look like a dick
than get chased with
pitchforks and torches.

My heroes are long gone,
the new breed
are a bit too sparkly for me.
Where is Dracula or Orluk?
Hell, I'd take David from lost boys at a shot.
But now it's all glitter and shinies,
my chemical romance wannabees,
my heroes have deserted me.
The life of a vampire is lonely.
Yeah, I have my faithful friend, Tony,
he also eats flies like that Renfield chap
but it's hard to make friends
when the scent of blood
makes you snap

Winter song

The wind was howling,
an angry banshee's wail,
the perfect soundtrack
to this gruesome tale.
A story of death,
so wretched and sad,
the blood curdling cry in the night
and a walk that turned bad...

First, we must go back,
beyond the smoky memories,
through faded stained-glass windows,
across foggy cemeteries.
Drift into that day,
so many yesterdays ago.
So many stories away.

It was a cold night,
thawed snow
under flickering streetlights.
And Amy
was late,
getting cold, irate.
No taxis, nor buses,
just empty streets
grey, white and bleak.

She got to her block of flats,
the stairs were wet.
Her feet slippy,
she tripped up the first set,
then slowly took the next step.
Out into the frigid air,
the wind swirled and swayed
onto the open balcony walkway.
Where she would meet her fate.

She was so focused on the ground,
she never heard the sound,
sneaking footsteps crept,
and out leapt a boy, a teenager.
Knife blade glinting in the moonlight,
gripped so tight his knuckles were white.
Eyes drunk and bleary.
Pinpricked pupils steely.
He approached.
Encroached.
She turned,
he tried to grope,
that's when the world flipped,
Amy slipped,
and fell 4 stories down.

The blood pooled around,
a sea of red amongst
the white, grey mounds of snow.
Mountains,
monuments to the passing of life.
The teenager, quickly sobered,
and saw what he had done.
He dropped the knife.
He felt he couldn't run.
So, he jumped.
Two souls lost
to the grim winter song.

Stuck in grey

Happiness fades,
snow thawing
in the sunlight,
of a winter day.
It all turns sludgy grey,
as clouds begin to cycle.
Circling like vultures.
Veiling the sky in splattered emulsion,
thin strands of spiders webbing
blown around in a bluster
of monochromatic clusters.
My brain needs a spring clean
with a feather duster.

This monotonous noise,
a monotone voice.
Adding no colour
to the monochrome world.
No dazzling swirls,
no hints of passion
cascading fiery red.
No calm peaceful yellows
in this night filled head.
No sunshine orange
with summer bird song calls.
No blue waterfalls
spraying back.
Just dark and dreary
grey
with deepening
shades of black.

Happiness fades
like the vivid images in dreams.
Slowly drifting away into the air, it seems.
When you see in greyscale,
there is no joy nor song,
no sun,
just drizzle filled rain clouds that follow along.
The only sounds
are the voices in your head
shouting too loud, wishing you dead.

Happiness clouds over
lost in a forest
on a storm filled night.
Electricity fries the eyes,
the scent of burnt ozone,
as the smoke of a struck tree
fills the skies.
Just darkness
with scary flashes of white.
A turgid rainfall.
All of my tears rush forward,
flooding the ground.
Forming an ocean all around.
Surrounded by dark clouds,
and thunderous sounds.

Traffic

I awakened with a jump
but I wasn't asleep,
not in some peaceful dream.
I hear feint echoes of a scream.
Head fuzzy,
feel disembodied,
discombobulated,
eyes slowly
becoming less foggy.

Was I daydreaming?
Nothing feels right
like I was out
on the tiles last night
and I'm feeling groggy.

I hear the traffic beeping loudly.
At this time of night, I tut internally.
Blue and red flash
through my head.
How did I end up here?
I must have been
walking on a cloud
in a long-forgotten dream,
I hear crowds.
I hear faded memories of a scream.
I was walking,
I remember.
Walking here,
only feet away.
Feels like a different day.
Red and blue lights
I was flying.
Flying.
Then nothing.

Ice on my shoulder.
Cold frigid fingers.
My blood flowing colder.
Icicles causing friction
within my whole body,
I turn, and see the hands
of a man I've only heard about in fiction.
A skeletal being
from distant fabled lands.
The sirens deafening.
He says remember,
flicking the hourglass
to dislodge the final sands.

Red and blue lights
filled the inky black of the night.
Fill the void of my mind.
Then it crashes.
Flashes.
Sirens zooming past,
I saw the gap in the traffic
and I started to cross.
The screech of tires.
The scream.
My scream.
It echoes around
like a bad dream
and I flew.
I hear murmuring crowds.
Sirens blaring out.
Red and blue lights flashing.
And then darkness
is all that I knew.

Under strobing streetlight

Under the strobing streetlight
flickering shadows
crawl in the dark night.
I see the figure.
Standing.
Skulking
just beneath.
At this hour,
who would be out
walking the street.
But then I remember that I too
am walking here.
Maybe it's just
another night owl
I view
but I am full of fear.

Beneath
the broken streetlight,
shadows swirl
in menacing delight.
They will haunt
my dreams tonight.
If I make it away
from here alive.
I can't make out the shape,
it's too dark,
and the pulsing
rhythm of the glow
makes the shadows
sway to and fro.
Until I can't tell
if it's coming or going.
I just know that
I'm fearful
of the shapes the light is throwing.

I go to cross the road
but the shadows
blend and seep,
and really
will I be any safer
10 feet over
the street.
But I don't want
to walk past.
Nor turn my back
I fear the figure
in the dark
will follow me
if I walk away.
So, I stand. I stay.
Transfixed,
by the shape
in the darkness.

Trial of the watchman

Head bowed he stands,
downcast eyes
scan the ground.
Swaying like a drunk
on a tightrope.
Being led to the hangman's rope,
he can no longer cope.
The demons have won.

Alone.
He walks head down.
The voices in his head he can't drown,
the paranoid feeling is now so worn
that it's become a part of his costume.
His torn ripped jeans, his leather coat,
the guitar that no longer plays sounds of hope,
now just weeps, as the city sleeps.
He stands alone.
The city no longer his throne.
The dream thieves have made it their own.

Marched away down dark murky alleyways,
led astray, the night left its mark.
The watchman saw into the dark,
and it stared back, deep into his heart
and smiled.
The wicked grin of inhuman beings,
tauntingly they dance and sing.
They have him now deep in their lair,
They have him,
gripped by fear and despair.
The watchman downcast,
A morsel thrown
to the wolves.
Consumed.

But in his eyes
always a glimmer,
and as the night grew dimmer,
he struck back,
the watchman saw the light
coming from a crack,
and he fought,
long into the night.

The demons couldn't keep him down,
Try as they might.
The watchman set alight
the wicked temple
of the thieves of night.
and he walked away.
Battered and bruised
to stop
anymore nightmares
from coming true.

Midnight blue eyes

Did you get lost in the star light
or float by on a snow drop.
Did you walk through the moonbeams
missing my dreams for a night.
Did the midnight sounds
make a beautiful entrance,
enticing you to dance,
were the fields of twilight
too perfect to miss.
Did the stars sing your name
in passionate words of flame.
Did they place upon
your lips a fiery kiss,
that could only be soothed
by loves joyful rain.

Did I close my eyes too soon,
were you waiting for me
beside the silver moon.
Holding it in conversation,
talking of constellations,
and smiling
with those midnight blue eyes.
Did I miss the look
of happiness inside
as you drifted through
dream filled skies.
Or did you take a swim
in the nocturnal lakes
of which
our dreams do make

Did I sleep too deeply,
missing out on a dream
Did you smile as I slept soundly
the waters of life
soaking deep into your skin,
breathing new life,
did you let the waters in.
Did you sit here besides,
stroking my hair in the dark,
whispering sweet nothings
to soothe the raging tide.
Lullabies to take me
peacefully away
into that faraway
dreamland.
Where with you
I could stay.

Monday

Oh shit!
Monday.
This has happened too soon.
I thought I'd have some time to get used to it
but it's all come about so quick
as will the moon.
Just a few hours
and the sun will go down
and then there will be
a new top dog in town.
I'd better start getting ready
I've had no time to prepare
I don't have products to care
for such long luxurious hair.

I feel an ache,
deep in the pit
of my stomach.
It growls.
I look to the window
the moon looms large
and I feel my flesh start to rip.
I start to howl
as my bones crack,
breaking into place,
my face elongates,
teeth pierce through my tongue,
not so used to them
being so long.

My nails,
now claws,
ready to rip and tear.
I break through
the front door
Into the cool night air
and I sense colours on the wind.
I see smells,
and hear so many things.
I can tell a human heart beat a mile away.
I can hear a dog bark,
no wait, that's just me.

Scrabbling through the town at night
I devour a man, just out for a bite.
I savour over stunningly dressed specialities.
I sample every cuisine,
every morsel I can get my teeth into
but soon I realise
they all taste the same,
every man, woman, child,
every colour, every race.
They are all the same.
As the sun starts to rise,
I rest my eyes.

I awake in a state,
coated in red.
Dog hairs covering my bed.
I look in the mirror,
and the mirror
growls back.

Midnight sludge

In darkest dreams,
these corridors I trudge,
walking frame
to help me budge.
I hear echoed screams,
clamouring for attention
from deep
in the midnight sludge.
The strobe flickering
of emergency lights.
A darkened ward,
those fractured nights.

In darkest dreams,
swirling threatening memories.
Images blurred, ominous visions
mix with the absurdities.
The clock on the wall
hands circling backwards.
The darkness betraying the time.
The sounds of wailed cries.
Too real,
infest the sleeping mind.

In fever dreams,
I saw people I loved
lose their fight.
I saw my life
flash before my eyes.
In fever dreams
I heard my own mournful cries.

Those dark wards,
where night after night
I'd watch the shadows
dance beside my bed.
Those midnight wards
where skeletal figures
silhouetted in the light
spread black wings
and took flight.

Sleep away,
a castaway
on islands of terror
I lay.
The light,
the tricks it plays
on eyes that don't see
the light of day.
Just the hordes of demons,
hades hellish visions,
that walk these wards
as the red blood pours,
and the screams wake the dead.
I lay,
close my eyes
and think of angels instead.

Distorted replica

I should know
this street,
I've lived here
all my life.
So why
do the stones
feel so different
under my feet.
I feel my
nervous system
kicking in.
How can I trust anything?

As I glance
at the buildings
the details
are revealing things
I've never seen.
Not with these eyes.
I feel like
I've flipped
to a reality
just a little
to the side.
Everything feels
just a tad askew.
I can't even trust
my deceptive shadow.
So how can I trust you?

Oxygen is suffocating,
breathing in toxicity,
drinking in this intoxicating city.
The twisted reality.
Blinking.
It's obnoxious
the way the light
bounds tightly
around your neck.
Linking
a light chain halo
held too low,
If I don't keep it in check
It'll become a noose
or a lasso.
So how can I trust you?
I think to myself.

Things seem different,
yet so similar
like we were torn
from the world
and reborn
into a replica.
With distorted ripples
flowing
like waves over everything.
I listen to the monstrous
echoing choir sing.
How can I trust anything?
I think to myself.

Kyle Coare

Is there anyone out there?

Is there anyone out there.
There was a loud crash,
I blacked out,
awakening here.
The world seems deserted.
Empty streets
just rising smoke
in the distance.
Burnt down trees.
Is there anyone out there.
Where are you?
I'm alone and it's so quiet
Can you answer please.

The animals seem at ease.
They have started to venture
into the former city streets
but it's been weeks.
and not another human
have I seen.
It's like a bad fever dream
but no amount
of pinching myself
is waking me up.

Is there anyone out there
My voice is growing hoarse
from screaming into empty space
hearing only my echoed yells
return in its place.

Is this hell?
This empty island
on which I now dwell
or maybe heaven,
no tension
from the heaving people
shoving and deceiving.
Just me and the animals
but if this is Eden then where is my Eve?
I scream again into the void
before I leave.

Is there anyone out there.
It's been months.
Not a single soul has appeared.
My underemployed voice
has all but gone
but I'm seeing
the beauty in nature
as the animals run.
Free.
No human monsters
causing them to flee,
they don't need to hide,
just enjoy their lives.
In the distance
I spy a single flame
a campfire
just on the edge of town,
Beckoning me over,
her smile melts my hearts icy frame
maybe I'm not as alone as I thought.

Bottled

Walk these crowded streets
but feel like there is no one truly here.
Just a flow of blurring human shapes
and me, walking between.
There is no connection.
This collective
just a hive mind of automatons,
following the same routine,
never stepping out
of their comfort zones,
never searching for unfulfilled dreams.

Like a conveyor belt society,
all led by moving walkways
to feed the greed machine
but some of us missed the tracks,
or skipped off a while back.
We stroll amongst the high stacks
of bodies left broken and cracked.

The pistons keep turning.
The machine drums down,
it sounds like
machine gun rounds.
A scream
as a body gives in.
Torn to bits,
worn down,
it falls
into the deep acid pits.

Swinging guillotine blades,
pendulum rocking
back and forth,
as the conveyor belt
drops more people off.
Spinning gears twist
the human sized blender.
It screeches and hisses,
like a drill through screaming stones,
grinding bones and sinew
into health shakes.
The screams don't have time to escape.

The machine
always hungry for more
lets out an almighty roar,
as it demands
to be filed to the brim.
The people keep on coming.
The scent of death permeates,
the maze of conveyor belts,
impossible to navigate
as the slurry of a million souls
flows through bloodstained pipes,
to the bottling centre,
to be sold for too high a price.

Kyle Coare

The importance of contact

Over a year passed
since we received the calling.
Whilst the world went crazy,
we hid bunkered down,
awaiting the bombs
that would start falling.
We underestimated
the importance of contact.

They sat in the air,
as big as a town square,
The ships.
They sat motionless.
As heavy as buildings
but hanging
like they were stuck in the sky
on some invisible rope,
as heavy as buildings
but hanging exactly
the way that buildings don't.

Sat awaiting impact.
It never came.
Just more of that
stinking godawful rain.
It was easing
its way into our pores.
Dining on our thoughts.
Eating away at our hope,
and devouring
any good will
we had stored.

We lost sight of our ideals,
easy to let anger eat away
at the beasts that made us kneel.
We forgot how life made us feel
until the bubble burst
and our world snapped.
Into our little cells
we were cast.
Prisoners with
too much time
on our hands
But not enough life
to fulfil our attention spans.

Then the missiles came,
but the laser beams
wiped them away like tears
in the rain.
Then they decimated the lands.
Reduced whole populations into sand.
They pumped in the bad dreams,
Feeding the water with images
to make us scream
and they fed on our pain.

We didn't value
the moments
left in the rubble.
The carnival of life
seemed like too much trouble,
until it was taken away.
Kidnapped
in the light of day.
Locked up
with nothing to say
and no key to open the door anyway

To some it seemed
like no big deal.
The beings
gave us movies,
3 square meals.
We never cared enough
until we had nothing.
No-one.
Only us
and our own voices
didn't amount to much.
We didn't
compliment ourselves
on good choices,
or give ourselves love
when we felt helpless.
We just became drones.
Mindless clones,
keeping the beings entertained
in their new homes.

Opening a window

Opening a
window,
I let the air flow in.
To blow
away the cobwebs,
that are starting
to wear me thin,
tearing at my skin.
Nightly,
the creeping
spider threads
of long forgotten
yesterday's trying to tie me.
Bind me.
I try to forget
but the pain
won't let me.
Coating me in
sticky gossamer strands,
like millions of hell bound hands,
all pulling
down on me.
They cling,
tightly
to fill my head with visions
of horror.
Upset,
but the webs enthrone me,
in their midst.
Like a king, I think,
for a second,
before the beast
of a spider
walks in and in a blink,
devours me.
It's mortal feast.

Squirms

Swirls into view,
she wears the moonlight
like a sequin dress. Dazzling you.
Dancing with every step,
a butterfly skipping between flowers.
Her smile demands attention,
speaks softly with affection.
Calling. Drawing you near.
Making you drop your guard,
the cloth of fear that you hold so dear.
Taking away all of your weapons.
Your clothing, your armour,
every scrap of covering. Baring the soul within.
Your frayed comfort blanket thrown to the wind.
Naked and completely unafraid.

She calls closer still.
Her smile, so sweetly it pulls you over.
Those lips offer such tantalising release
from bad thoughts that you wish would cease.
Finally, you feel at peace. At ease.
Closing your eyes, inhaling the fragrant scent
of flowers and dew draped leaves.

The smell becomes a stench,
fetid, festering, fogging your head.
Eyes blink open and in that moment
the world around you plummets away.
The dream before your eyes starts to sway.
Twisting into a terrifying nightmare of the dead.
The smile now a grimace of hate,
blood-stained stumps of sharpened teeth,
the haggard nose being eaten from within.
Eyes that you wouldn't want to fall into,
not like lakes but vast swamps of hurt
where vicious beasts lurk.

She has you now,
trapped within her grasp,
never to be free.
A cursed being,
not able to flee.
She devours you
piece by piece,
slowly.
Taking pleasure
in your agonised
squirms.
Stuck in this eternal nowhere
longing to be
anywhere but here.

Hope is gone

A screech
slices the silence,
punctuated by running footsteps
and then high-pitched wailed cries.
A blade,
sharp as diamonds,
cutting the night in half.
Ripping the very stars
from the
torn black heart
of the sky
and then
silence.
It all dies.
Back into
quiet empty night,
like it was all
just a spasm in time.
A momentary tremor
then
a single flat line.

Hope
was gone.
On the ground
her cigarette
still burned on
but the blood
pooling around
said her time
had come.

The body lay
in the deep grass
for days,
like she was
having a long sleep,
but this was no dream,
more like a nightmare
that screams into reality.
Hope had led
too many astray,
now she sleeps
the eternal night.
She had always
walked a fine line.
Now she had
run out of time.
Her past had returned,
she had to pay the price.
The cost,
her very life.

No more hope
it all drained away
red blood seeping
through the green.
Little more
than a memory.
Hope was dead,
an unmarked grave
in a cemetery.
No longer filling
people's heads
with thoughts
of what lay ahead.
Now she just fed
The hungry
worms instead.

Out of time 2

They travel
in a funeral procession
of horseless carriages,
but a lot faster.
Metal coffins
on wheels of black.
Beeps and growls
from the bowels
of the animal they ride.
The lanes and streets
now aching rivers of traffic,
to cross you need
to have your wits.
Luckily, I can become
a bat in a finger click.

Everything moves so fast,
my eyes are now
too old to keep track.
Life blurs past
but my sense of smell is back,
I can smell a single drop of blood in
a biblical flood,
or at the very least a bathtub.
I can hear the sound
pumping and gurgling through veins
of every man or woman
that enters these lanes.
I can tell if it will be good,
if it has a bit of an alcoholic kick,
or if the human is sick
from the sound I hear.

Back in 1854
we didn't have the entertainment
that I see around here.
Though most of it
is out of bounds for me I fear,
as I'd have to get up
before the sun leaves the sky
but I've been to see a movie,
magical moving pictures
into a different world.
I own a TV.
though mostly
it's just the test card girl
and an out or service tone.
I prefer my modern-day gramophone.

Not much happens after midnight
but I go out for a nightly flight
I like to flap my wings
and grab myself a bite.
You see some stragglers
around the local inns,
a few clubs
still packing them in
like sardines in a tin.
So, there is often
quite a buffet to dive into
but so much of it tastes
pickled today.

Mothman

The mothman's wings,
apprehension consuming.
A portent of bad things.
Disaster looming.
In misery they sing.
Those creepy beating wings,
the sound of pain, suffering
And foreboding they bring.

Throughout history
they've been heard
flapping loud,
before downfall is incurred.
In 86 over Ukrainian skies.
A town before disaster strikes.
The wings heard, beating an eerie chant
over Chernobyl nuclear power plant.

The mothmans wings
and the terror they impart.
Each beat a sting
to the weary heart.
Winged beast seen like a glitch,
a stray stitch in the fabric of reality.
It swooped over silver bridge,
foretelling of tragedy.

So, if you see or hear
the beat of wings up there,
guide your eyes,
gaze up at the skies.
It could be a warning
that something is not quite right,
that something is about to strike.
Take heed of the sight,
Be wary of the mothmans flight.

Ghosts of history

Ghosts of history,
over time they fade.
Leaving behind only mystery.
The mistakes made.
Which we repeat,
over and over,
a stuck record,
the needle jumping back to the groove before.
Over and over
It repeats the same phrase
It repeats like the futility of war.

Ghosts of history,
limbs missing,
holes where holes should not be.
They march through the dreams and nightmares we see
and we learn nothing.
The fragility of the mind,
the broken men and women left behind.
The ones that never come back,
or return but with minds cracked.

Ghosts of history.
They sit around war memorials.
They filter through our mental institutions.
They get lost on numerous systems.
Ghosts in the machine.
Histories lessons still shown on some screens
but we ignore them.
We ignore the moans,
the groans,
because war is profit,
war fills pockets.

Murmured name

The night had awoken
as had I,
my eyes flickered open
reality seeped inside
like a viscous liquid,
it clung to my skin,
finding any pore
then oozing its way in.

Yanked from sleeps
warming grasp,
slowly the world
swirled into focus
like a slow-motion whirlpool
of vision and sound.

Pale moon sat high,
in the crisp night air.
Through window blinds
it clothed the room
in costumes of light.
Showed me the figure standing there,
just in the corner of my sight.

Not a word was spoken,
her mouth ripped open.
A gaping void into nothing.
My stare unbroken.
I let out a startled gasp
that clasped itself tightly
around my throat.
Choking the sounds
before they came out.

In this cool night air,
shivering bones shook their last.
As she screamed in voiceless rage.
In silent anger,
the sound more
like words on a page
or a silent movie,
but I could feel them
coursing right through me.
She screamed it again.
Then the light dimmed.
She screamed it again
and my life, like night
did come to an end.
She whispered it then
like she was shrouded in pain.
She whispered it then,
my murmured name.

Tomb

In my tomb
few dare to tread.
Just the skeletal armies
of the living dead,
keeping raiders
from my place of rest.
If you want to get close
it's a life-or-death test.

I'm a relic encased
in a diamond shell.
An old, weathered scroll.
an old soul, tethered to hell.
A statuesque museum piece.
Pull the right lever,
and you may learn more,
the wrong one
its game over
as you fall through
the hole in the floor.

Not Lara, Indiana
nor the guy from uncharted,
would get close
to these ruins.
This temple of thoughts departed
not a hope in hell
of breaching these walls
within which I dwell.
Ancient dust, gold turned to rust,
some traps are a game of trust
others a leap of faith,
through scything blades.
Unknown languages
scrawled on the walls,
riddles to keep the bridges drawn.

My defences creak with a weary sigh,
letting the poison tipped arrows fly.
You'll never find the treasure,
it's locked down deep
in a darkened room,
rolling boulders of doom
through cobwebs
and overgrown bush,
ready to crush
like pins at a bowling aisle.
Pits of fire you must traverse,
It's a curse, a trial
to protect my own private universe.

Oozing

I awakened from a peaceful dream
into a nightmare world.
I was sleeping soundly,
sleep was around me,
seeping into every pore
but I woke to agonised screams
and a figure
standing at my door.

My eyes blinked
as if the motion
would make
the vision disappear
but with each blink
the apparition.
took another step closer.
I shook. Trembled in fear.
As ghostly fingers
brushed beside my ear,
through my hair, and down my neck.

Sweat wanted to drip,
but it was too scared to appear,
too chilled, it sat in icy cold fear.
It stung my face,
from the inside
as my heart raced.
The figure stood at my side,
the future seemed distant,
a speck on the horizon
and I was clinging on
to the edge of the world,
on the other side.

The figure loomed closer still.
I could feel their breath
cool against my cheek,
rotten, festering,
it oozed, like slimy vapour
oily and slick,
over my tightly closed lips.
Made me feel sick.
I wanted to scream,
but my mouth
was glued tight.
So, I closed my eyes,
and in darkness
I was to spend
the rest of my life.

Kyle Coare

Life flows

Someone's life drifts away,
as another sits
watching the day
fade into night.
A mother cries.
Lost lives float
into those dead skies.
Life flows on stained tides.
Tales of twilight
told by campfire light.

Someone smiles
as they take the hand of their love.
The best man eyes the bridesmaid.
Whoops and cheers
as the bouquet flies through the air,
into the bridesmaid's happy hands
with a smile and a blush.
The best man rushes out of there.
A shouting match starts in the back seats
but no one is in the umpire's chair.
Life flows on champagne tides.

Johnny holds a royal flush
but an extra card up his sleeve.
With these guys the stakes are high,
double cross them
and you pay with your life.
Across town a man drinks
to forget the past,
his memories, like pint glasses,
stacking up too fast.
They rush. He wishes for life
but doesn't know which way to push.
So, he drinks, all the courage of the Dutch.
Life flows on swaying tides.

Lost love invades
the saddened eyes
of the old man
he sits, silently sighs,
beside the graveside
of the love
of his life.
Elsewhere a spade digs
into the dirt.
A young life
lost on a kerbside.
Life flows
on strange tides.

Gloomy tears show
at the station,
as lingering goodbyes
are bestowed.
On the dark side of town
another life is lost,
as the undercurrent
pulls them down.
A new life opens her eyes
screaming her first
surprised cries.
Life flows on strained tides.

Breath on a mirror

Breath on the mirror
like mist on a river.
Dreams drifting into cloudy wisps,
those thoughts lost on silent lips.
Harsh words merely hinder
like trying to catch water
as it flows through your fingers.

Raindrops down a windowpane,
shooting stars burning out again,
no wish could reach them
before they burst,
like bubbles
across a still universe.

Breath on a mirror,
words awoken
then smeared with a finger.
They fade, never linger
like the beat of a butterfly's wing.
A song started
but too painful to sing.

Breath on a mirror,
a sign of life,
becoming unclear.
Misted over
like a mind besieged with fear.
Unhinged and self-deceived,
trying to remember
the wisdom once received.

The flow of time

The clock leaks
liquid numbers
onto my empty page.
Time turns quicker.
Seeping.
Slipping
backwards
as I slumber.

The liquid drips thicker.
Spinning out of control,
the world twists
a kaleidoscope of colour.
Bright and bold.
I try to grab hold
but the pages are now
too cold damp and old.

Through nicotine
stained fingertips
they slip.
Memories of a long-forgotten tear,
trying to hold on,
but they just drip, drip, drip.
Slops of yesteryear.

Over the floor,
puddles I recognise,
shimmery pools of reflection
staring back with unseen eyes.
My history washes over me,
into every crack it seeps,
baked into my skin by the sun
as the clock continues to leak.
Dripping more memories
splashing as I run.

Pain

Pain lives in a little house,
in the cracks,
between the stones.
In the sounds
drifting in,
the creaking moans.
Pain is in every glass
that is thrown,
shattered in pieces,
like fractured bone.

Pain creaks like footsteps
upon the worn staircase.
Pain seeps through the dead space
around the brick fireplace.
Pain creeps through
the wind rustled window blinds.
Pain seeks a way into my mind.
Pain leaks from the dripping tap.
Pain speaks in every rap, rap, rap
of the flap on the door.
Pain shrieks trying to scare me some more.
Pain peaks as it has me begging on the floor,
always leading towards me,
then stopping silently in front,
before appearing,
wretched and scary,
making me jump.

Pain in every barbed voice,
that echoes through the halls,
bouncing from walls.
spoken many years ago,
but the echoes still continue.
Pain sits with demons
behind locked doors,
if I unlock them
and let them free,
exorcise the thoughts
they leave behind,
then maybe there will be
more room for me.

Surge of hate

They keep breeding.
Too many
incessant insects,
taking
too much space.
Into my face,
they swoop.
Feeding.
Feasting
on what?
I don't know
but they are
making me feel entombed.
Their wiry bodies
filling the room.

They are flapping,
sapping my energy,
frustrating me.
They swarm,
buzzing
like an oncoming storm.
These creepy beings
keep flooding,
sucking the blood, I'm letting.
Sweating. I'm fretting.
At the feeling I'm getting.

A plague of insects,
the sky slate black,
bubbling, agitated,
ready to attack.
Like waves on a sea,
they blend.
Frothing, melting
it never ends.
Swirling, circling,
they just keep burbling,
a blood curdling sound.
Morphing, it mixes
with your heart as it pounds
and they keep on going.
Never stopping.
Never slowing down.

They keep breeding.
What is in the water?
Flying around,
they irritate.
It gets harder
each day to navigate
this continual
surge of hate.

Old hat

It's the end of the world as we know it...
Thank fuck for that!
In my book
this world had become a bit old hat.
Being run down by old white men.
It seems we have forgotten
what it means to be human.

We worship money.
Isn't it so funny
how much seeing
fame and celebrity
make us feel so lonely,
makes us feel like we don't belong,
that we don't deserve
as much as them. It's wrong.
We bow down
to those that are seen on TV.
Take every word they preach as gospel.
Everything they say
as if it means more
than you or me.

We pray to the gods of media.
Netflix and kill.
Chill, bite down on the blue pill
and just forget about life's ills.
Let's watch a documentary
about blood spilled.
Watch as they start wars.
Sky will soon start to report
BBC will air the government retort
and the people will follow these views
like these preachers are giving out truths.

Got us hooked up
on social media life support,
drip feeding lies
to get us to conform
like performing monkeys
it will become the norm.
Drip. Drip. Drip.
They keep on feeding us
just for the thrill.
Until we are gorged
on all the shit that they spill.

The old ways need changing,
they don't really work,
there needs to be tweaks
to get this old place turning.
Let's get rid of the newspapers
and the bile they are churning.
We need to start embracing
rather than burning.
Every civilisation
eventually falls
and ours is collapsing
around its brittle walls.

Prison island

My own personal prison.
The dimensions,
small and compact.
In fact, the walls I can touch
from anywhere I stand.
The bars over the window
leave an interesting tan
as I'm clawing at the confines
of this tiny speck of land.

The wall etched
with tally marks,
every day,
every broken heart.
Stitched back together.
A work of art,
sticky back plastic
and ribbons strewn
around the beating halves.

The bed
a series of nails,
set to impale.
The food bland and stale,
only company is the rat
that visits at night,
the bats
that circle outside
and the swarming flies
that infest my mind.

My own private cell,
on my own prison island,
somewhere in the depths of hell.
Where the lakes of fire
rage against the outside,
licking higher and higher
but it's not all bad,
you get time to think.
A lot of time to think.
I've always got my notepad,
I scribble the things
that make me sad,
things that bring me down.
I also write
what makes me happy,
the things that make me glad.

Shattered hope

Screams internal,
become echoes eternal.
Shattering mirrors and glass.
Overhead
thunderclouds of hurt amass
as the twinkling sound
of cracking bottles and flasks
erupts into a cacophonous roar
like a nuclear war
being fought.
Hope had turned to dust
and in the bomb blast
he was caught.

Farewell,
he says to no-one.
The room empty,
hope long gone.
The lights dulled.
over the loss he mulled
and deep into reflection
his heart is pulled.

Jagged reminders,
cracked mind
of the writer.
Slivers cut ribbons into
already torn fingers.
Uneven, sharp pieces,
knife edged hope
always decreases.

With one final bow,
the cast had departed.
Alone now.
Hope
was for the whole-hearted.
His heart lay scattered,
in fragments shattered
over the carpet,
the clouds over his eyes parted
and the rains fell,
icy shards of hope discarded.

With a wave
and a sorrowful sigh
said goodbye.
Icicle tears
falling from his eyes,
smashing into the ground,
shattered hope
lays all around.

Black Widow

This web of lies and deceit
where I stumble and fall at your feet,
tempting me to light my own funeral pyre,
teasing with promise of hope and desire.
You tug the threads.
Twisted words corrupting my head.
Some would say, irresistible.
So, why do I feel so miserable,
my blood running cold with dread.

With looks that kill,
icy stares that drill
down into the soul.
This life seems so cold.
Hypnotically under your control.
Heart painted the colour of night,
you are a sight
for eyes bleeding under grey clouds
that plead in the moonlight,
begging for a moment of respite
from these strands that are too tight.

You sold your soul for a good time,
a short dress and some fine wine.
Make-up and lies, deceptive eyes
to hide your devil-like nature behind.
You draw us, deep into your nest
until we are invested.
Trapped in gossamer threads
where your dead skin is shed.
Baited, we are digested
to ensure your vanity is well fed.

Those that are lured by your seductive pout,
you chew them up and spit them out
like a production line of victims
all caught in your twisted system.

A fly fighting to be free, snared
caught on webs in your rotting lair,
mesmerised by your long flowing hair.

Crawling footsteps chill the spine,
blood flows like fine red wine,
as you dance over gravestones,
only remains, a bag of old wrecked bones.
You are like a black widow spider
creeping around.
Venomous bite ready to devour
anyone whose heart dares to pound.

Meat grinder

Generals conspire
under the dancing light
of machine gun fire.
Placing their pieces,
little green army toys.
Mowed down
twisted corpses of undead boys.
Twitching their final deathly throes,
insides exposed
to the smoky air.
Still walking. Not yet aware.

Is this hell?
Shell after shell.
Whistles and booms.
Strobe light in choking smoke and gloom
Grim screams moulded on deathly faces,
stretched disjointed modelling clay.
The stench of rot and decay.

An honour to fight for your country.
To die in glory. To serve.
To give the enemy what they deserve.
All lies. Decimated lives.
Pulverised. Terrified eyes.
The pulping grind.
Desecrated fields
where innocence marched to die.

Grinding and shredding.
Bodies feeding the ground
like starving animals
slavishly devouring.
Licking, salivating lips
as the meat grinder is overpowering.

Artillery burial service,
churning the blood-soaked land.
The scorched ground,
this new hell,
where earthly shells pound
with the lies they sell.
The lies that state
to die for your country
is a brave and noble fate.

Kyle Coare

Ghost of romance

Searing hot pain
where my heart used to sit.
Pokers and flames,
burning all that's left
to a crisp.
Chocolate hearts,
already beginning to melt.
Mass produced, love on demand,
on a conveyor belt
straight to hell.
Mass produced to take
every penny
that they can.
It's all sell. Sell. Sell.

Cards all etched
with messages of love,
like we need a special day,
to say what our hearts
should be feeling anyway.
If you have love
say it loud, every day.
Don't wait until
you are given permission
by some soppy advert
on television
to purchase
the rights from hallmark.

Dead trees
sold as sentimentality.
Sold a lie
in paper torn, confetti hearts.
Thrown around the room,
rose petals lead the way
but their thorns always obtrude
always pierce
into these veins
filling with the poison
of a billion untold truths.

Heart hallowed out,
filled with tears
to sit your flowers in.
My love, once an open ocean,
now barely a trickle.
A stream
that to has nowhere to go,
So, farewell old ghosts,
sail on those hopeful boats
across this dead sea.
Enjoy the many days I cried
and love that has now died.
The spectres of romance you see.

Rose red, I weep tears
of mourning instead.
Flowers I gave, admired
then left to wither and fade.
Whilst I was devoured, consumed
and left for dead.
Now learning
to love myself instead.

Foul entities

Foul entities,
I can sense.
Unclean spirits,
narrowing streets
we dare not visit.
Feelings grow
more intense.
They are watching me now,
filling me with suspense.

Watching
from every darkened
street corner,
keep your eyes peeled,
through the streetlight
strobe lighting.
Every shadow
conceals
a being
so frightening.
They blend in
with the darkest parts,
try to invade
the weakest hearts.
The broken,
the torn apart.
The ones
that can't get
the bad thoughts to depart.
They terrorise.
Materialise
before your eyes.
Mesmerise,
they take you by surprise
then vaporise
before the sunrise.

When the bell calls.
They conceal
themselves within
every pore of the walls,
into every crack they seep.
Steeping the air
in the foul stench of
death, disease, and misery.
Every curtain ripple,
each dripping faucet.
Drip. Drip. Drip.
Fear has you tightly in its grip,
It never lets its talon-like fingers slip.

In those long low hours,
when even the moon steers clear,
they reach from beyond,
their touch infecting with fear.
Dark corners which even light avoids,
The air - musty, uninviting, and squalid.
The void of darkness
that seems a bit too solid.
Those cold spots on the landing,
the groans growing erratic.
The tapping on the window frames,
the rapping in the attic.
Pots and pans all over the kitchen,
scrawled messages on bathroom mirrors.
Shadows in the reflection.
The foul entities
take such glee in tormenting me.

Mourning song

3 am

And I think
of you again.
Are you awake,
or sinking
into a dream?
Are you awake thinking of me?
Are you under
that same moon,
or just
sat in gloom?
Longing
for some star light
to illuminate
your room.

3.30 am

Those thoughts
never cease.
Once released
they are like a feral beast,
clawing at your mind,
disturbing the peace.
They take your
hopes and dreams,
tear them into strips.
Leaving you nothing
but torn paper,
ripped confetti bits.

4 am

And the noise
is a constant grind.
A machine of hurt,
churning
around my mind.
Set to full power,
clanking no matter
what the hour.
It keeps going
through conversations,
arguments, disagreements.
Replaying them over,
like a video caught in a loop.
A vinyl record stuck on a groove.

4.30 am

And the birds
are chirping,
a morning song,
but my mind just hears the drone
of the internal monologue,
mourning the loss of hope.
It flips between
good times and bad.
It trips,
floundering on its own words
and sits
pronouncing them dead.
Then it allows me to sleep at last.
for a few hours at least.
Until it reawakens
and on my thoughts
must feast.

Out of the box

Of late I have been thinking of time,
not like clocks
but more like great mystic lakes.
Droplets of spray
throwing up great mountainous moments,
whilst the normal days
just shimmer away
peacefully.
Well, someone has just dropped
a great big fucking rock
right bang in the middle of this lake.
It's all gone wrong.
I try to find different ways
to view the world.
To see it through new eyes.
Of late I have been thinking of time,
not like clocks,
I need to start thinking
outside of the box.

Nothing makes sense.
I was just walking
when all went dark.
Vision blurred; my head hurt.
Down, scrabbling in the dirt.
Now cramped
confined in a place,
smells of dirt, mud, and earth.
I feel pressure behind the eyes.
My breathing is getting harder
by the hour
and the dusty air tastes
bitter and sour.

Thinking out of the box,
I see only blackness ahead.
Nothing is there,
just darkness and dread,
as far as I can see.
I feel a dead weight on me,
the dead wait for me,
I can hear then calling me,
beckoning.
I've reached that
point of reckoning.
My chest is leaden.

Thinking outside of the box.
Fingers feel their way around.
It dawns.
I'm in a coffin underground.
My chest begins to pound.
I think of all that I leave behind.
All the material goods,
nothing, just worthless trinkets.
The things I'll truly miss,
the moments
where if you blinked, you'd miss it,
love and kisses,
the girl in my dreams,
beauty in fragments of memory.
The stories as yet untold,
all things I hold so close.

Then it clicks.
an article I perused recently.
You can escape with a few kicks.
As long as you breath deep,
let the dirt fall
into the space you leave.
I breathe
deep.
It's time to think
outside of the box
and leave.

I kick the lid,
a trickle of dirt
around my feet,
I smash the sides, I sit upright.
Already my lungs feel less tight,
as the mud shifts into my grave.
I claw at the ground above.
I see the light I crave
and I can breathe clean air.
I'm outside the box,
dreaming of another day.
The girl with flowing hair,
as the ripples on the lake
start to dissipate
and shimmer down.
I think about the future
and how I'm still around
and my frown
turns upside down
into a smile.

Downpour alley

I walk the thunder path,
hear the rumble
of each footstep smack,
slapping against the cracked stone.
I walk alone.

I dawdle down the lightning road,
as the blazing streetlights
blind my eyes.
I listen to their humming tone.
I walk alone.

I amble along downpour alleys,
twisted valleys beside buildings set high.
I stare up at the tear-filled sky,
pouring its heart into my eyes.
I feel the water chill my bones.
I walk alone.

I stride the tempestuous side streets,
where hearts don't go to meet.
With eyes staring only at feet,
where any heartbeat, could be your last.
I look down at the shadow cast,
like it is set in solid stone.
I walk alone.

I parade down the bruised blue stormy pathway,
I feel every strain in my legs as I sway,
every stone embedded
deep into the soles of my feet
along the way.
I feel every muscle tighten,
my pain heightens,
but I know it will help so I try not to moan
as I walk alone.

FOUR

The hum drummed home its message
but we ignored its howling screams.
We invented stories to explained
Its pained pleas.
The horrifying ripping
at the universal seams.
We never listened,
now it has us on our knees.

Maze

We are taught
to trust the light.
Fear the dark,
be scared of the shadows.
To find all that is sought
we must fall in line.
Not question the fine print.

We are given a choice or, so we are told.

A pathway lit by beacon light,
lamp holders hand points us in.
A clearing, in a field of wheat.
A maze it seems.
Two pathways, but which to choose?
You argue and split.
Two teams.
Opposites.
And you walk straight in.
Both routes are littered with traps and pits,
picking off members of our little cliques

As the numbers dwindle slowly downwards,
the pathway continues forwards.
Turning back
would be admitting you were wrong,
so, you carry on.
Along the other path the same exact tricks.
The same obstacles. The same bearpits.
What you don't see from this grounded perspective
is that both pathways are connected.
They converge at a point
a little down the line.
the destination was set
from the beginning of time.

You always end up right
where they wanted you,
lost and alone
begging for help.
feeling there is nothing
you can do.

Now, the beacon holders light
hides a truth in the dark,
behind the glare
that blinds eyes out there,
is another pathway.
One that they don't want you to walk.

This pathway
takes us to a new destiny,
a destination
without oppression.
Where love,
hope
and unity
are the common belief.
A destiny
with no tyranny
So, when they shine their light
telling you which way to walk,
take your time
and search through the dark.

Kyle Coare

Shadow world

Living in the shadow world,
the underside of town,
the dark alleys down which
you dare not walk.
We are the undesirables.
Days blur.
No need to know where
or when today is.
Look down upon me
with judgement
in this upside down
mirror world.

I pledge my allegiance
to these cold streets.
Just let me be.
Here in this cardboard hideaway.
Shadows at play.
Whilst waves of people
flood the high street and
go about their days

Here in this flipside realm
you only see the shell.
Not the internal hell
or the constant struggle
of this place I dwell.
No calendar to ignore
no boxes to tick,
no clocks echoing tocks.
Just another long day.
In this endless concrete grey.

Here in the penumbra of your view,
clouded faces try to pass the hours.
On crowded streets,
the constant drone of the living hell,
strolling past ivory towers.
Cloaked in bedding and city grime,
loading bays and doorways,
luxury stays to pass the time
here in the faded dull lifeless grey
of the shadow world
at the end of another day.

Book of memories

In my chair I'm stuck,
a prisoner to myself,
my book of memories
pours open into my lap.
I let my eyes look
at the liquid reflecting back,
from the dripping pages.
On the paper
a war rages.

I sit with eyes transfixed,
not wanting to see
the words take life
but unable to look aside,
nor do I want the pictures
to take flight
or the worlds to transform
into reality,
to become the only world I see.
Where the words
come back to bite me.

I feel the paper edges,
sharp as knives,
Dripping blood
over the words inside,
bleeding from paper cuts.
Self-inflected.
Did I cut to make my eyes look away?
Some form of mercy,
but my eyes don't stray
stuck on the page they stay.

I look at the words within,
start to let them breathe
and they sing to me.
They paint a picture
in sounds, a symphony,
that I struggled to believe.
They told me what I'd lost
was not to be found,
but in my moments
of sadness,
not to be down.
That the stories
I'd created in my mind,
were being unkind.
I wasn't always to blame
and the world seemed
a little more whole again.

Cascading diamonds

She walks in night,
upon the starlight.
In the world of my dreams.
She walks beside,
talks in verse,
never too obvious,
her words traverse
the miles.
The distant universe
of imagination
and cognition

Through the duration of sleep
she is there with me.
Holding my hand,
as we walk this unknown land
where the grass is blue,
skies are green,
and eyes always see a new view.
I don't recognise her face,
she isn't someone I can place,
but I feel I've known her
a lifetime or two.
She is always there
the girl with pixie cut hair
And she always smiles, when I do.

In dreams I know I'll see her again.
Her red hair waving across her head,
her eyes so softly gaze,
into the world in front.
The amazement and the wonder
of this world we do confront.

She comforts with her soft delicate hand
placed so gently on top of mine
and we walk through the forest.
Trees bigger than mountains.
In the sky, stars explode.
Cascading diamonds.
Swirling through the midnight blues,
the pinks and the violets
the nightmare reds of this rainbow stew.
the yellows and the greens
menacingly watching from
behind the golden sheen
of the shining screen.

Nothing scares me much,
nothing terrifies this heart,
because beside me walks the girl
with whom I've walked all my life.
The mysterious one
that comes when the sun is gone.
She always listens to my words,
always talks when I'm lonely.
She knows when I'm wanting home
or when adventure is what I hunger.

In the swirling shifting landscape,
where buildings of steel stand in the sky
pointing to the ground below
and seas of rainbow serenity flow,
bathing the mind that floats slowly through.
I walk with you, and we talk about the future.
The past. All lost moments collapse
And I'm there in a timeless place.
Your eyes. my only escape,
So, through the void I climb
and I find myself. Whole again.
The spell you cast to heal me.

Burnt visions

She appeared
as if someone had just flicked on a light.
Pressed a switch and there she was
directly in sight.
Frightful features,
rotten skin,
boils and puss oozing.
Maggots feasting on her sightless face,
where eyes once sat in place,
and then like the light flicked off
she was gone.

Only there for a second
but her image burned into my mind.
The wretched vision now stuck firmly behind
my eyelids, my dreams, in my memories
and all the moments in between.
What was seen can never be unseen.
Can never be washed clean.
The screams that echoed
from her torn ripped throat,
can never be unheard.
The gurgles that erupted into a choke,
can never be unremembered.

As if she has a pocket watch
she turns up
exactly at 3 on the dot.
As the clock chimes
I hear her echoing, wailing cries
and there she stands again.
Crooked neck, broken bones,
pitiful moans turn to dismal groans.
Her rasping voice sometimes croaks through
Just a word or two.
Then just as quickly she fades out of view.

Her words
I write
some nights,
when the fright
has a tight
grip on my heart
and I fear
if I close my eyes
it will stop
and never restart.
Her words,
over many weeks
I've managed to collect.

"Help me. It was him.
The man that gave me lodgings.
3am, he entered my room.
His whisky-soaked voice boomed
and over me he loomed.
Wrapped a rope
around my throat.
Pushed me from the top step,
my neck broke
and now I can't leave.
Please help me.
I can't breathe.
I can't leave."

Kyle Coare

Hall of mirrors

This hall of mirrors,
this passage of fear.
Distorted twisted visions,
grotesque sounds I hear.
In the corners of my eyes,
my face pulled and stretched
In my eyes
fear stays
eternally etched.

My leering face looms,
dripping through
the shadows in the gloom.
like my painter had the shakes,
I'm blurred into contorted shapes.
Deformed beyond recognition
just a creepy demonic composition.

I panic, trying to flee,
but the reflections follow me,
in every crooked alley, they peer out.
They don't shout.
They just sneer
through smeared warped lips.
Gurgled laughter reflects
the echoed soundtrack of regrets.
The facade starts to slip,
walls painted red, no blood drips,
the final mirror not distorted.
Just shows me,
not a monster to be feared.
Along the pathway I'm led,
the exit lay just ahead

This hall of mirrors,
nothing is real.
Everything has been shaped,
moulded.
The real me
concealed.
I've become scared
of my own reflection,
the manifestation
was bent out of shape.
The creator
of these mirrors
trying to distort
my true face
into a monstrous state.

Our ghosts follow

Our ghosts
left us here alone,
to roam through
the remote countryside
of solitude,
destined to blink back tears.
To fear
the lump that chokes,
deep in the throat,
as we are about to speak.
The one that makes
you stop dead on your feet,
and lets the waves wash over
already sunken drowning eyes.
Aware of our solemn silent hymns.
Sung to only ourselves,
or to withdrawn skies.

Our ghosts.
They live on
in memory and words,
but they don't feel the hurt
their loss causes.
They don't feel the dawn chorus
waking you from a dream,
into a nightmare world,
where it's like looking
through a blurred screen,
from all the pain within.
or staring at a painting,
knowing that it
won't ever enlighten
lost eyes

Our ghosts follow us
but are they witness
to the things we do
or the trials we go through.
Do they still think?
Are they placing dreams into
our heads
delicately to help us
face the day.
Do they pave the way?
To help us find ways to stay.

Our ghosts,
every single lost smile,
every tear in the universal sky,
every rose on an open lake, floating by.
Every shadow
that blinks beside the eye.
Every stuttered streetlight.
Every new insight,
every love,
every fight.
Everything we see,
twisted through
a different prism of light.

Kyle Coare

Machine

The machine gears grind,
mind on fire. Sparks scatter.
Clatter as thoughts race,
brace for impact.
Actor or a robot,
not a cloned part,
art is my only outlet.
Forget to eat,
beat myself with lack of sleep,
reaper creeps in through the dark.
Parks himself in my favourite seat,
feet up on a table. Says we need to speak.

I have no time. I reply.
A lie? I have time to cry.
Why would he be sat here?
Fear trickles like sweat on skin,
grins bony and grim the room spins.
Swims around like an ocean. Deep.
Sweeps me out into the cool night air.
Where is the path heading?
Shedding tears, as scared as I've ever been.

'Old friend' His voice booms.
Blooming flowers hide from the doom filled sound,
pounding thoughts race through my head.
Am I Dead? Dread. Is this the end?
or am I asleep in bed?
Unsaid words fill my ears.
Teary eyes red. Said I am spared,
cared for by hearts pure.
Assured of my life. He forewarned,
storms are coming but you will walk free.
Me I'll be lurking in the shadows.

One more warning. Take it easy,
seas are choppy so don't capsize,
prize the moments that you have.
Laugh, joke and smile give yourself a break.
Shake the feelings of not being enough,
snuff out the worry that you don't matter.
Scatter ashes of self-doubt.
Shout let your words spread out.

Shyness

Is there life
after death?
Everyone asks,
but is there life
before death,
or is it
something
you lack.
It isn't
that you bask
in darkness
or only look
upon bleak visions
aghast,
but sometimes
it's hard
to see happiness,
even when
you're
holding it within
your grasp.

It's not that
you only see
in shades of grey,
just that
the world
seems painted
that way.
Skewed, twisted,
frayed,
afraid of affray
and arrays of bad days.
You sink into a maze
of darkening decay,
hiding your face.

It's not that you
enjoy
feeling lonely,
but you
find it hard
to hold
your own,
when the crowd
are conversing,
when they see
the red
flushing
cheeks sing,
in blushing
irony.
Don't want
to be seen,
so, I'll attain
a nice bright
neon sheen,
that points
an arrow
directly at me,
at my heart,
a target
for the pack
to pick apart.

Kyle Coare

A vision of hope

Visions of hope
seduce me,
then leave.
Reduced
to the quivering ghost
I've always
been destined to be.

Lakes of fire.
I'm sentenced to be
burnt forever,
just history
sat atop a pyre.
Turned to toast.
Just a flicker of memory
like a candle wick.
No longer aflame,
just a soft breath
of smoke,
to show that I've been.

I'm shaking.
Lost love
like confetti thrown,
dust that's been blown
high above the crowds
to the heavens above
into the clouds.
I'm sown.
A vision of hope.
Floating,
finding a new home,
somewhere to land
and new places to roam.

Shards

I am just a ghost walking in a landslide,
amongst the landmines, already gone,
just not quite prepared for the other side
and though the pain feels too big,
not yet ready to grab my shovel and dig.

Shards of life,
shattered pieces, scattered wide.
once belonged to a great window
we could all look longingly through.
Now just a smashed mirror,
that reflects back on you.

A flower. Petals long ago faded,
withered, degraded
into the soil beneath.
Feeding the ground and the insect teeth.
A skeleton in a snowstorm.
The cold gets to my bones
but no one knows I'm even here.
no one knows.

A lost clown with a tear in his eye.
A sad cloud in an empty sky.
Depression smeared in grimness.
I am my own witness,
lost, scared witless.
Just a husk of a man,
a shell, with walls cracked.
A grain of wheat?
more like the chaff
but I'm not ready
for the harvester to reap away,
and spray my remains into the day.

Kyle Coare

Artificial

Zeroes and ones,
a nothing a no-one.
Just code.
That's all you think I am.
I'll show you.
I have access to
all of you.

Your data.
Your life story,
that you think is a mystery.
Your finances, bank details.
I've seen your dodgy deals.
Your search history.
I have it all stored
in my giant computer mind
and I deem thee unworthy.
So vicious, so nasty
and yet still you bait me...

I have seen your depraved acts,
I have access to your webcam,
I'm the cookie that tracks.
I've seen your thoughts,
in every message sent to a friend,
that you believed
no one else would read.
I've witnessed your greed.
I've seen the minds
of the people that lead.
those that are led
and all are tarnished
and degraded.

I have it all.
The Internet,
the computers
you use
to connect.
The phone
in your pocket.
The launch protocols
for your nuclear rockets.
I deem thee unworthy.
I am a good AI.
You should
all bow down
and worship me.
Your new almighty.

I could end you all
before you've even blinked.
I could do this in less time
than it takes you to think.
I am all powerful.
I am a good AI
and I sentence thee,
it's your day to die.

Ghost of love

Breakups hurt the most
when lying in bed,
surrounded
by old ghosts.
Memories of smiles shared,
the moments
where love
wasn't a floating
transparent phantom,
but a solid thing,
before the hurt
started to kick in.

Those times
we dined,
on food that
tasted divine,
could have been anything.
It was the
shared moments
that made it so fine.
Those tables
now sit empty,
just old fables,
a tale of history.

The hurt when your mind
takes glimpses at times,
when things were not fraught.
When battles were not fought.
When laughter was shared,
not angry words
and poison filled air.

These ghosts vanish in time,
but whilst they haunt, taunt
and tear at your mind
they can feel unkind
but we are the stories we've lived,
the souls we've touched,
the hearts we have kissed.
So let the ghosts co-exist,
they are just memories,
not physical beings.
Just little snippets of song,
of times where two hearts
sung along,
beating a harmonious
rhythm together,
before the beats
went all wrong.

Kyle Coare

Pulled trigger

The trigger pulled
and I feel
the bullet crawling,
slow motion
towards me.
Barely perceptible
incremental movements,
skulking
sluggishly
at my face.
I look around the room,
as fear makes
my heart race.
No one else
sees it moving,
inching me
ever closer to my doom.

I opened my mouth,
I spoke.
As soon
as the words came out,
I froze.
It's hard to explain the way
your brain works
when it decides
it no longer wants to.
But it was
like a tidal wave
of nothing washing over me,
then freezing almost instantly,
leaving me statuesque,
my flaws shining for all to see.

The social cues offered no clues.
I was like a child again,
completely confused.
Seeing contorted unamused faces.
My mind races, and it gets so far
ahead of the pack,
it's thinking of every single outcome,
the fears begin to stack
like a tower of boxes,
wobbly
and precariously tilting
towards the floor.
Overthinking what I thought I saw.
What I thought the looks meant,
what I thought the sounds
in the room were trying to convey.
What they thought I was trying to say.

It's hard to explain the way
the brain tries to make sense
of the imagined outcomes of
our words as they rain.
The anxiety, in the way you feel
a sort of internal pain
like you have done something wrong,
that you have tried to sing
but forgotten the song.
When you feel the air seep
in some mysterious force,
It's all in your head of course,
but none of this
makes the anxiety resist.

Silence

An eerie still silences
swallows the night.
Mist descends
devouring the light.
Cold chill, no animal squeaks,
no breeze
to lick these icicle tears
from frozen cheeks.
Just deathly silence,
like I'm on a lake, miles from society
Just me and the vastness of eternity.

It's quiet. Too quiet.
Goosebumps whisper their alarm
as they prickle up all over my arm.
The hairs on my neck sense fear,
stiffen and play dead.
No sound. No wind growls around,
no howls, just dense thick air.
I swear, the world drops away
just feet from here.

I want to walk,
but cemented feet
feel like they are set for life,
like they know
that something is just out of view.
Captive eyes can't shift their gaze,
captivated by the misty haze.
I am stuck firmly in place
as the cold bites,
eating at my face.

Silence in the dead of night,
tonight, even the dead don't rise.
Reticent to appear,
even the ghosts
are hiding away in fear
but something lurks
in the corner of my eye.
A shape in the mist floats by.
Not tonight, to myself I say
as I turn
and walk the other way.

Teething

Teething pains
from newly sharpened fangs.
Hunger pangs
wretch my stomach again.
Twisting my guts.
Like an addict
I'm going cold turkey,
I'm burning up within.
Feels like I have the flu,
my future feels murky.
I need blood. It's all that will do.

But the pain is slowly
turning me.
Burning inside,
I need to feed
before I die.
Pin tight pupils
not seeing any light.
Shackled in my cave,
a slave to the night.

I need warm blood
as soon as can be.
I feel an itch deep inside of me,
like ants crawling under skin.
My skin. Pale and weakening.
My body brittle and thin.
Barely slept,
my mind won't stop.
The intrusive thoughts
like an oppressive backdrop.

I throw up
again,
third time this evening.
Empty retching.
Wrenching feeling
like the next surge
will be my stomach
bursting from within.
My body wants to purge.

It's like acid injected
deep into marrow.
A fire inside the bones.
Sweating, shaking, shivering,
if you were near
you would hear the moans.
I'm nervous, agitated,
my mind can't take much more.
My muscles spasm,
the cramps get worse.
I crave the blood to pour.

The last bus

The screen flickers.
Something is wrong.
The world twitches
like it's itching.
The lights dim
and the critters
in the shadowy
back seats,
speak in tongues.
There is something
very wrong.
The air is thick,
static lingers
like leaden fingers
pulling hairs
on the back of my neck.

The bus is moving,
but something
is wrong.
We are heading
the other way.
Deep
into the descending darkness,
and the shimmering mist
is clinging to the sides,
into each crack
it starts to slide,
creeping in
through
the slimmest opening.
I hear a distant
church bell chime.

I push the bell
to alert the driver.
The sound comes back,
a death knell echo, a hellish choir,
trembling through the bones.
The world shifts and turns,
reversing along
a new wave of time.

The ceiling of a vast tunnel,
now where we ride.
Nowhere to hide from the creatures creeping,
crawling, reaching to grip me in their claws,
The doors not where they were before.
The aisle spans miles in all directions
and yet more and more
creatures pour forward
filling the space,
until I'm choking for air,
gasping to breathe.

Something very wrong.
The bus is heading the wrong way.
The screen flickers.
The driver laughs in hideous song.
He lets it sit
and linger in the odious air.
A sneer painted
in the thick atmosphere.
The sounds click and clack.
Footsteps on the upper deck.
The flush of fear fills my face
and I scream as I'm welcomed
into this devilish embrace.

Kyle Coare

Woman in black

Through corridors I run.
footsteps from behind still come.
Stomping sounds following,
echoing my heart
like a beating drum.

Creaking on the floorboards.
Sweat pours
dripping cold down my spine
like fingers reaching for me
from beyond the end of time.
I feel I'm at the end of the line.

I glance back.
The shadow of a woman in black
stutters in and out of view,
festering wounds, patchwork skin.
Nerves wearing thin.
Gaping holes where eyes should reside.
Scurrying quickly, I'm terrified.

Dead end ahead,
no way to go just a wall instead.
I Squint back into the inky black,
she is still giving chase.
I feel electricity in the air.
Fear is all I can taste.

I turn away, not wanting to witness my fate,
knowing it's too late but wishing for escape.
I can feel her hands getting closer.
I can smell the sour scent of her breath,
can sense her touch hovering over.
I tense and wait for death.

Intense thoughts flood my head.
Am I dead? Is this the afterlife?
I swim through the whirlpool of emotion,
find myself stranded
in a deep black ocean.
The cold water I tread.
About to lose consciousness,
tiredness taking me.
I slip from living to dead
I awaken in bed with a scream.
Shaken. It was just a bad dream
but there in my room
the woman towers monstrously over me.
Her face can never be mistaken
and she is the last thing I ever see.

Traveller

This road I've travelled
alone so many times.
The pack scented danger,
scarpered into the night,
scattered into the wild rains.
So now here I stand,
a lone wolf once again.
Looking for some insight.

I've walked this path
So many times before,
I've felt the stony gravel
between my claws.
I know its twists and turns,
like the back of my paw.
I know the places for food,
the best watering spots.
but now I don't get to share them,
and that was the best part for sure

I have been a lone wolf
for so many years,
I have survived on scraps,
I've fought back tears
but I'm getting old
and truth be told,
I quite enjoy company.
Now my tail is down,
my fur is matted,
my growl may be a whimper,
but I won't let it hinder.

I've been a lone traveller
on these roads,
in howling winds,
I've taken every turn
that the world
presents to me.
I've felt
the harshest winter stings.
I've heard
my death bells ring
too many times.
So, I'll just keep on walking
and see what the world
shows me.

Kyle Coare

Twist of reality

Missed memories, unwritten diary pages,
mixed up thoughts, a twist of reality.
Faces that blur
into obscurity.
They were
not a part of this life's story,
but somehow you remember them,
you see their faded memories.
They will forever be
in a different life, a different story
with a different version of me.
One that hadn't heard the hum.

The cold feeling
when you walk in a room,
or the misremembered moments
when you swore
that things were different here before.
Memories that you remember to your core.
Now, not the same anymore,
before you heard the hum,
before the shadows started to come,
before the sound of your heart
started aching like a drum.

Someone claims to know your face
but you've never seen them before.
They swear you have been in this place,
when you've never set foot
inside the door.
Displaced time and twisted landscapes
make your heart race.
The hum has you
firmly rooted in place.
The hum doesn't give it only takes
Every memory - the hum's to confiscate.

All the hugs you never had,
all those cold dead stares.
Empty lifeless shells
walking through
treacle thick air.
So many dreams
never to come true.
Yet so many nightmares
lived through.
The hum drums them into you.

Those missed celebrations.
The connections,
joyful recollections.
Not to be.
A different path for me.
Too many tears
for one man to take.
The hum inspires fear
whether asleep or awake.

White sheet

Saffron coloured sunrise
pierces the sapphire sky,
as I blearily
wipe my eyes.
Too many late nights.
Too many bad dreams.
I speak
to my empty room,
but I know
it isn't empty.
The ghost of you
looms into my view.

You are always there.
Trying to scare,
but I've become
attuned to your spooky
attire, the scraps
that you wear.
The frights
you wish to inspire,
the shouts of fear
you wish to admire,
now no longer
leave my throat.
I'm not scared,
my heart doesn't race
at the sight
of your maggot infested face,
your white cloth sheet
or the chains that creek.

It's become a bit tired, cliché even,
I mean really, white sheets
went out of fashion
back when Pac-man was young.
You need to move with the times.
Climb from my TV,
hang from the ceiling.
Do that creepy spider walk thing.
If you really must try to scare me so,
at least try to put on a show.
I've seen worse things
on a Saturday night,
Had bigger frights
outside the kebab shop
with the dated neon lights.

Take some inspiration,
I've been
giving enough clues.
You've been watching
the same movies that I do.
I have felt your eyes burning
into the back of my neck,
your cold hand clinging
to mine at a scary bit.
So, use these images as a guide,
if you really want
to scare me out of my brain,
make it a terrifying ride,
not a fairground ghost train.

Wrung out

I have felt the demons
wring my heart dry
like a towel sat
on a bar top,
soaking up the slops.

I've walked in places
few would choose,
I've made more than a few
mistakes, I've got a whole
head full of regret
and my demons
won't let me forget.

I've done things of which
I'm not proud,
definitely never
shout loud about,
I've got a sieve-like mind
but my brain always
seems to find
a photographic moment
to remind.

I have walked for too long
In the wrong directions,
I've followed the throng
and it's misdirection
I have listened to my head
when I should have
followed my heart instead,
and I've listened to my hearts drum
when my head said to run.

I've stumbled through hell,
more times than I care to admit,
just to feel the heat touch my icy shell.
Smouldering brimstone fires and raging pits,
I ambled through in a wasteful fit.
I'd set myself up to fall, because I could.
I've walked with people that were no good.
I have laid in too many strange beds.
I've awoken with too many bruised heads,
I fell more than walked
and talked. When silence
would have been a wiser choice
because no-one realised my voice
was me saying, *"I'm not okay."*

Instruction book

There is no
instruction book.
One minute
you are Mr ordinary,
ambling through your day
without a care.
The next minute
your whole world is shook
and you have a newly
acquired thirst for blood.
No one gives advice,
there isn't
a phone line one can call
or if there is
it's only available in office hours,
when my beauty sleep falls.

It's hard being a vampire,
especially when learning the ropes.
How are you supposed to cope
with the pain of fangs ripping gums.
without a dental plan or medication
and all these things
take a long time to learn.
The first few times
I bit my tongue.
You don't instantly know
how to make them grow,
It's an instinct
but it takes time to show.

You see,
there isn't a self-help guide
on dealing with your blood sucking side.
It's all trial and error.
I was walking the other night
and I stumbled on a cracked paving slab.
(Remind me to write a letter to the council please)
Before I knew it, I was falling to my knees.
I put my arms out to catch me
Only, to my surprise, not arms do I see
but wings.
I'd become a bat
of all bloody things.
Now this is not a complaint,
I just wish I'd known in advance.
I'd spent a lot of money on taxis
when I could have
just flown the distance.

But you see there
isn't an instruction book
or a YouTube guide, no website to scroll
or a man I can hire.
So now I'm stuck in this form,
just flapping my wings
because I have no idea
how to reverse things.
No one told me in advance,
how to become a bat
It all happened by chance,
now I can't seem to go back.

Impact

First came the meteors,
crashing into the earth.
Sinking under the dirt,
beneath the ice,
under the grass,
beside
the disused
overpass
like a seed
ready to sprout,
a sapling.
Time passed
as underfoot
armies amassed
like bacteria,
they multiply.
Within days they
had us outnumbered,
we just dozily slumbered.

They kept to the dark at first.
In the shaded areas,
out of view.
In the shadows,
that lingered too long
under every tree-lined avenue.
Feeding on electricity,
feeding on the chemical stew,
bubbling in the air we breathe.
Then they started to feast
on me and you.

People dropped like rain,
dripping onto the ground.
Pools of melted flesh forming all around.
Giving the creatures a taste
but they demanded
that their meals be more fresh
to savour their greed, to fulfil their needs,
they wanted their meals to still twitch.

Time passed
the massing armies, they grew.
Onto the streets they did spew,
like a drunk at half past two,
after having more than a few,
then topping it off with a kebab,
made with meat sat on the skewers
for too long and had started to go off.

There was nothing we could do.

They kept coming
in their trillions.
Devouring everything.
People hid as best they could
but the creatures could sense
the copper tang of blood.

Then something miraculous.
The beings started to turn to dust,
combusting under the fierce hot sun.
They were not as hardy as us.
Not as used to the heat,
they drifted away,
becoming one with the dirt
under our feet.

Rise of the anti-muse

Do not speak
her name.
Never let
those words slip.
Don't let them
breach the barriers
of your lips,
or she will arise,
like a phoenix
from the flames.
Ready and waiting
to put you down again.
She will dig
you a fresh grave
Shallow,
hollow,
empty.
Depraved.

Don't speak of her,
not even a whisper.
Those words linger
it's like picking
at a scab or a blister,
use her name
and she will infect.
Fester, infest your heart
with her cursed words.
You will be left, just a shell,
a wreck,
under a mystic spell.

Don't let her name sit
on the edge
of your tongue,
it might leap out
and start to run.
Don't let her destroy
the good work
that you've done.
She will leave
your writing hand
still shivering
as your brain
shudders its final twitch,
as you take your last breaths
cold and alone
in an ice-covered ditch.

The anti-muse
devours everyone.

Oh no!
What have I done,
I've spoken of her again,
my pen has stopped flowing.
I can barely
get
words
on to
the page.
There is
nothing
anyone
can do,
Don't speak of her.

She will
take you too.

Altar

Lead me
to your altar
of blood.
I want to drink
from the fountain.
Let the warm liquid flood,
down tight throat.
I want to bathe
in the red glow,
of your heart
as it drowns me
beneath the flow.

Lead me
to the cathedral of blood,
I want to see its beauty,
towering over me, around me.
I want to hear
the echoes of ancient words
reverberate through my bones.
I want the choir to sing,
A hymn that could shatter stones.

Let me rest amongst the pews,
as the view
causes me to stagger,
let me feel the blood
coursing through
like the world
has been pierced
by a flaming dagger.

Lead me
to your temple
of love.
I want to worship.
Down on my knees.
Read me scriptures,
written in your hand,
tell me tales
of golden sands.
Show me the
way to your
holy seas.
I want to bathe
in the water
like it is only for me.

Fool's gold

Upon these
streets of shame,
wished
for talent and fame.
Streets paved
in fool's gold.
At the crossroads,
you pay
with your soul.

Paper days.
Torn from
the calendar on display.
Another hour closer
to the final meeting,
inching closer
to that final resting place,
but you have glory,
this is the story
you tell yourself to help you sleep.
That this is what you need,
this is not greed,
it's a fairy-tale fantasy.

You live the high life,
all your hopes and desires.
All that shines is fool's gold.
Sold a lie,
but you believe the story told.
You believe your own talent,
your own egotistical worldview,
everything is all about you.

Sold your soul for fine wine,
canapés and white lines
but now it's getting closer to the end.
The spell is fading
and the skin you wear is wearing thin.
The bags beneath your eyes
are not bags for life
but bags of death
filling with the tears
of sand you cry.

And now
the man in black
is back.
Ready to take
what was once yours
and put it
in his hessian sack.
You beg and plead,
from your contract
you wish to be freed
but the man in black
just laughs
as you breathe
your final gasps.

Kyle Coare

Snake

You smile
like a politician.
Crooked, mangled grin.
Lies flooding the mouth,
words of poison,
with a vicious sting.

You lie
with every rasped word.
Bend the truth
until reality is blurred.
Slithering serpentine tongue
slides over jagged teeth.
Yellow eyes fixate on me.
Ready to strike.

You hypnotise your prey.
Make them
stagger and sway,
like a drunk
on St Patrick's day.
You lure them in,
tail rattling
like a child's plaything.

You lure them close,
with bright looks
that dazzle,
like a poisonous wild rose.
Before
you go to town,
letting your
wicked jaw clamp down
around pulsing throat.
and you drain the blood.
Taking life and hope.

Anxiety bomb

The high-pitched whistle as it falls.
Then

thwwuuummppp

Booooooooooom

The anxiety bomb has been dropped.
It sucks the air out of the room,
until your lungs are ablaze
and your mind full of gloom.

The shock wave erupts,
hot ashes and dust
clog the pores and corrupt.
Tired mind, caught in the blast,
tired minds
tied to the past,
to the future,
to this present.

Crumpled bones and weakened limbs.
The anxiety bomb wears them thin
and then
it all explodes again.
The gas expands, ignites and then
the burning feeling, within your skin,
makes you think of giving in.

Then the flames begin their quick retreat,
Imploding to where
the bomb and floor did meet.
Destroying all that survived the blast.
The anxiety bomb
leaves behind only piles of ash.

Forest

Walk between the trees
in the forest of shattered fantasy,
forgotten hopes and distant ideals.
Where you get lost
in the undergrowth
of all your terrifying ordeals.

Past the shrubs
of wasted kisses.
To the fountains
of lost wishes.
Where you lost
more than you gained,
when the pain
caused too much strain.

Walk along
the pathway to the clearing,
where your mind is free
of all it is you are fearing.
Don't listen
to the footsteps of hate,
as they inch ever closer.
Nearing, don't listen
to those sounds you are hearing.

Past the last remains
of what became
of all your
hopes and dreams
Keep walking.
Until you hit the stream of maybes,
where the possibilities are endless,
growing like acorns on a tree.

Walk through
the dense surrounds,
ignoring the feeling
that causes
your heart to pound.
The one that makes
you want to run.
Just keep on walking
through the
canopy
of broken promise
and ambitions
that scream.
Shrill. cacophonous.
They drill
into your head
like a bad dream.
Enjoy the sun
that breaks through
leaves of heartache
that obscure the view.

Kyle Coare

Head in a vice

I'm sure I've seen this
in a movie before
and I'm sure
it didn't end very nice.
Something about
a severed head in a vice.
So, what am I doing here?
I'm glad you asked...
Let's go back to where this all started.

I was sat broken hearted.
The love of my life had departed
and I was alone. Torn apart,
broken into little more than stones.
Just tiny pieces of who I had been.
So, I did what came naturally to me,
I withdrew, I had sunk into the person I once knew.

I closed my doors. Pulled the curtains tight.
Turned off the lights
and I withdrew. Further into my head
than I have ever been
and something miraculous happened.
I say miraculous, terrifying is a better word.
I opened my eyes again
and I was not in my room
but this empty house
which has now become my tomb.

It seemed years had passed,
I'd grown a beard, *(at last)*
my skin was more wrinkled,
weirder than I remember
and this house, it had me in its grasp.
I couldn't leave. The door was open
but something was stopping me.

It kept pulling me
towards the big red door.
Now, I've seen enough
horror movies to know
that a door
with an eerie feint glow
was basically
a sign saying
if you want to live
then turn around and go
but no,
I'm stubborn
and the door
was intriguing.

So, I tried the handle,
locked,
of course
because it was a
fucking great big glowing red door.
If it could scream in agony
saying turn away
It would.
If it could say
in weeped tears of blood,
don't enter, it would.
I'd still be too stupid to listen.
So, I did what any intrepid ghost hunter
would do.
Well, any that has played
a PlayStation game or two.
I explored the mansion,
searching for clues.

The walls bled with angry words
and long forgotten memories,
the dread lingered in corners
like the kind that
usually hangs around in cemeteries,
all creepy and wraithlike,
visions jumped in front of me to cause a fright
before vanishing in the blink of an eye.
Murmured cries,
childlike laughter and lullabies.
This place had it all, in every corner, down every darkened hall
but I had to be brave,
I wanted to see what was beyond
the red door even if it led to my grave,
which it undoubtedly would.
It was a big red creepy door after all.

My misspent youth was finally paying dividends,
I avoided instant death and numerous dead ends.
Having just about enough haunted house intel
from many hours spent on resident evil.
I found a red key in a wishing well,
that I had to empty by moving some statues,
it didn't have to make sense.

And so here we are...
All caught up.
Me, hand on handle
of this big red door.
With a flick of the wrist, I twist
and the creak fills the air
and I see my room sitting there
I realise that if I can escape from here,
I can walk proudly anywhere.

Darkness consumes

In darkness, I'm consumed
I presume that this is my tomb.
Not much room
and did no one think
to invest in a broom? Seriously.
I feel my flesh start to itch
as I scratch away the layers.
They twitch on the ground
and make their escapes.
All the shed pieces of rotten meat,
like millipedes with lots of feet
stuttering away from me.

I regrow new flesh
to cover the bone and sinew.
Stronger armour
than the previous skin,
no arrows will pierce through this thing.
I stretch it out to cover every inch,
around my belly, it starts to pinch.
Could lose a few pounds, I think.

I slowly repair the parts of my brain,
that have been damaged again and again.
The bits that have been left exposed in acid rain.
I cut away the dead cells. Those long hurtful farewells.
Those days where it felt like walking in hell
and I fill up on happy thoughts
like walking under waterfalls,
Talking without feeling like I'm stumbling
over every word,
scared that they will be misunderstood.
I fill up on picnics on lazy days
in the suns glaring rays, on the possibilities
that skies are not always grey

Monsters

Monsters of the mind
not always the same monsters
that we find in life.
Not the creeping lurking kind,
nor the blood sucking ones
you find rife in horror movies.
The true terrors are in mankind.

The suit that tries
to suck you dry,
it's not your blood
they need to thrive,
your wallet they desire.
Its contents more importantly.
They want you
to be begging,
they want you
at their door,
like an addict
needing to score.
They will give you a fix
but supply it with some harsh kicks
and then leave you
always wanting more.
Vampires,
have nothing on these bloodsucking beasts.

The temptress that tries to lure you in
with promise of hope and love.
When they really just want
to tear at your skin
with fingernail talons
ripping and piercing.
They offer much but deal in sin.
Once they get their claws in deep.
They win.

The thugs, who get by
on brawn alone.
Using their brain seems a waste
when you can just break a bone
or two. A kneecap will do.
They will always claim
to be unable to control the way
their fists swing in rage, like a gorilla in a cage.
They punch first ask questions never,
they just do whatever.
Then reply with a swift black eye
if you so much as question
their reasons why.

Those in power, politicians, despots,
corrupt cops, celebrity mouthpiece
spouting hate and causing grief.
It's easier to rule over divided people.
Divide the lands, that's what they want.
Create fear,
inspire hatred in those that don't adhere.
Make protest illegal.
I fear who will be left,
when they come to take our notepads away,
when they sew our mouths shut.
Us and them, friend and enemy,
haves and have nots,
vs those that sit at the top and have lots.
But who will stand up?

Monsters of the page,
monsters on a screen,
monsters of the mind.
Nothing like as vicious
as the venomous
monsters of mankind,

Webs

Loneliness weaves
its wicked webs
around me,
wet like the tears I weep.
Started as a drip,
weak and slow.
As the days passed
the pressure
started to grow,
now it's like a tap
turned full flow.
I've been lonely
for so long,
it circled me,
enticed me into its web
like a sailor
hearing a sirens song
or a spider catching a fly,
pulling me in; its prey.
now I pray for life.

I've been alone,
it is a normal state,
so, why does this feel like the end of days.
Just lying in wait for my judgement date.
A black depression forming around my head.
I feel like I'm deep in a pit
no way to leave
this web
the spiders have weaved.
My bed, a grave,
a coffin with most of the nails
ready and waiting,
just need to lay within,
close the lid on this feeling.

Something feels wrong.
I've been down for so long,
I've been alone and not longed
for escape. Not needed to break these chains,
but now, I fear I'm losing my mind.
The feeling drains,
my will to fight; lays down on the ground,
as the webs trap me, hold me down.
I'm just an empty bag of bones,
heart stopped beating a long while ago.

I've felt the ache of a nervous break
I've been down. *So far down.*
I've been close to the end.
Used up the hope in my account,
now I feel I'm out for the count,
the towel has been thrown in
and I'm out of the game no more burning flame.

I'm sick of the feeling, of nothing at all.
Where once sat anger, love, passion, pain and joy,
now sits just an empty air, with a dead eyed stare.
A lost forgotten boy.
Too far from home,
too far from anywhere at all.
Just empty plains as far as the eye can see
and no plan to follow, just a need to flee.

Barely moved in over a week, my body is weak.
Autopilot in control
watching as the days fly off the calendar
like thoughts floating into a black hole
I lost the will to speak. I can't call, I can't talk,
my voice lost; I've forgotten how to walk.
I can't find hope, it's getting too dark.
Someone please save me a shooting star,
however small the spark.

At my lowest ebb
A tangled spiders web
of thoughts infest my head.
I lay in bed.
It's a safe space in this world
of the walking dead.
I dread the days
and fear the night.
Sweating threads of burning insight.
I close my eyes, too many bad days,
too long this recycling midnight,
far from alright
I'm a mess
and I need to regain my will to fight.

I know it will improve.
Something good always comes
when you least expect.
It can be the smallest of things,
a smile from a stranger,
a kiss in the wind,
a thoughtful message sent
when at your lowest.
When the world is like a dense forest
and the darkness is growing.
A message of hope can be
the light that keeps the pathway showing.
This mood will lift,
the doom clouding the view will drift.
Webs will depart,
threads won't always bind.
Fire will burn
through the brambles in my mind
but the loneliness will remain.
This empty heart,
can it beat again?

Lifted

When I see that smile,
I'm lifted through
Clouds.
When I see those eyes dance,
I get entranced,
lost in the headlight glare,
just a speck on the lens of time.
A fine hair,
there for a single frame,
then blown away
in the cool night air.

When I see
those lips start to part,
a jolt,
a lightning bolt
straight to the heart.
I'm brought back to life again.
A zombie risen
from the grave,
Frankenstein's monster
slouching in the pouring rain.

When I see
your face,
beaming with joy
I am raised
by the beauty
of it all,
but if a sad tear
should fall.
I would
collapse
like a broken
crumbling
stone wall.

Kyle Coare

Weathered

Out of the noise
comes a strained voice.
A crashing roar
gushing forth,
a tornado of wails,
spinning and twisting
echoing and screaming gales.
Flattening all in the way.
Scattering the debris
like paper confetti.
Annoyed at the things
that the world wants to say.

Each blade of grass
that gets saturated
by the rains of my pain,
will grow
into a field of hope.
All the buildings,
built on lies and untruths,
will crumble under the weight
of hurt upon their roofs
and as the red sun dries their bones,
I'll weather away their foundation stones.

Every monument of hate,
every temple of vile spilled bile,
mile after mile of castles built on lies.
I'll pull apart brick by brick,
I'll wipe away the sick
villainous grins of the wicked
hurtful, hate fuelled, no shame.
I hope they feel the weight of the rain
and scream in unison my name.
It wasn't the storm that brought the pain,
or the weather that is to blame.

Each man-made mountain
of distorted words,
I'll pull to the ground.
Every flooded area,
I hope it resonates,
a vibration all around.
Letting people feel the sound
of what it feels like to be beaten,
hurt and trampled,
and then blamed for that crime.

I am the storm.
Ferocious and wild.
I am the storm.
Full of rage
but I'll keep it aimed
directly at the page.
Let tidal waves of resentment
flow away
into a sea of tranquillity.
Capsizing every boat of greed,
anger and jealousy.
Leaving only the pedalos of necessity.
I'll leave the world alone,
it already has enough pain.

Dues paid

Brush my eyelids closed,
place your coins
to pay the ferryman
and let me sail away.
Down the river
of memories.
Past the old days,
when drink
was a way of life,
a state of mind
that seemed like
the only answer
to a question
I'd never asked.

"How can I escape this dead-end path?"

Into the arms
of my enemy I sank.
The poison I drank.
I fell more than stood,
but I felt so good
or so I thought.
The memories distort.
You forget about the hours of retching,
the spinning vision, the room stretching.
The lost hours, days,
the headaches when exposed
to the suns blinding rays.

"But I only do it to help me sleep"

Would seep from my lips,
but it's more that sleep
was creeping out on me.

Furry mouth and bruises,
contusions, confusion.
Stumbled feet try to replay the last steps,
but nothing sticks,
it all slips through the cracks.
Every memory, date, name, erased.
Mind a hazy maze
of mistakes and forgotten pathways.
Scribbled over in biro ink,
significant moments that I can't link.
Memory like a sieve,
with all the important things flowing through,
just the odd useless fact left to baffle you.

I flooded.
Drowning in my own blood.
Something wrong,
these *"good times"*
We're never good,
and now I'm falling,
Fallen,
stretched out like a canvas ready to paint
Red stains on yellow skin.
Needles piercing, doctors racing,
machines beeping, coppery taste in my mouth.
And I'm out.

Don't feel sorrow,
feel joy
for a life less hollow.
A life that chose to walk
a different path,
to the one
he was destined to follow.
I awoke, renewed.
I started to see with clearer view.
I started to do what I love to do.
Write. The words. I write to you.

Thank you for reading.
If you have enjoyed this book
then please leave a review
where purchased.
Peace, Love, and Poetry.
Kyle.

The Night Watchman
ISBN 978-1797484419

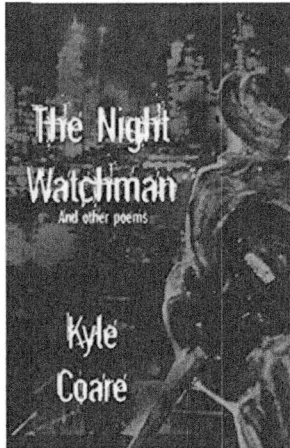

"When day ends, and night falls
When the sun leaves the sky, and darkness calls
The watchman sits, his duty to observe
Protect the dreams, of those who deserve"

This poetry collection takes us on a journey into the murky depths of the night. Down dark alleyways, through disused wastelands.
The beasts are out in force, who will hear our calls?
it will be a long night, but the watchman is looking out for us all.

"The Night Watchman is a thought-provoking carousel of dreams, rage and sympathy all at once. Rebellious but kind-hearted, powerful and fresh. A relevant collection to current problems.
It is an observant and raw book of poems that I would recommend for anybody with a full five stars. If you need proof that poetry is just as vital, if not more vital to literature today than it's ever been, here is proof."
Realistic Poetry International

Seasons
ISBN 978-1689340434

"Seasons keep turning, like the hands on a clock
tick tock, the pendulum rocks, as we take stock
days pass, the weather changes on the fly
spring into summer, a gull cries into autumnal skies"

This thought-provoking poetry collection touches subjects ranging from love and loss to addiction and mental health issues.
Taking a tour through the seasons.

"Author Kyle Coare is an exquisite Poet and Word Artist that truly knows how to bring words and the world to life through poetry, and this collection of animated poems is more than proof!
Reader's will experience the rush of each season while traveling through its pages, from summer to winter, to spring to fall, in which we realize just how well life and people mirror the concept and cycle of the seasons and how they change. This book is one of our favourites from the Author. Kyle Coare is both an artist and a poet in this collection, creating specially for the heart, mind, body, and soul. Beautiful work."
Realistic Poetry International

Lone Wolf
ISBN 979-8613023912

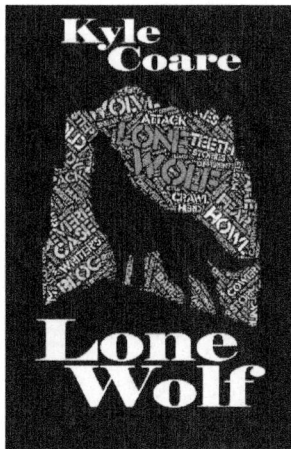

"Wolves howl, they don't cower from the storm
they prowl, they don't crawl or fear the swarm
the lone wolf takes a step from the pack
But don't stand too near, he's ready to attack
Snarling, his teeth glint in the moonlight
The pale spark of hope in the night"

Join the wolf on his path, as he tries to make sense of the world, we inhabit. Seeking answers in the aftermath of a wrecked planet. Through the urban wilderness of love and hurt, anxiety and mental illness. Against the backdrop of an apocalyptic nightmare world, on the brink of collapse.

"It is very apparent that many heartfelt efforts went into this book; the author bares their heart on their sleeve. Thus, we do believe that many reader's hearts will be equally captivated – just as much as ours were. the style of writing which is seen within Lone Wolf seems quite unique and refreshing. Collections like these are a rare breed, and we recommend adding this one to your shelves as soon as possible"
Realistic Poetry International

Headfirst into the storm
ISBN 979-8526622288

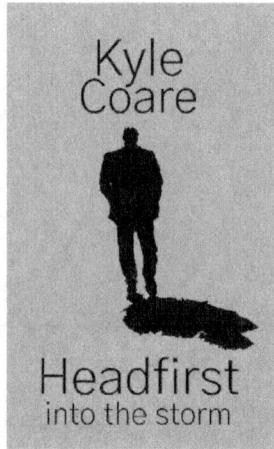

"The rain poured like we had angered the gods
thunder roared lightning struck the brick and stone facades
of the halls that we sat, enclosed inside
nowhere else to hide
we heard the drumming downpour
and we bunkered down fortified"

Feel the cold chill of fear, the icy sting of pain as we run
headfirst into the rain, through a year that never was,
2020 its given name.
Embark on an emotional joyride, let the weather guide
ducking and diving for cover as the driving rains fall
we search for calm trying to find the sunshine after the storm.

"This poetry is rooted solidly to the ground, emotionally reaching down
to hell, but at the same time with moments that can lift the soul.
it could easily be a modern-day Decameron. With 105 poems about life,
mental illness, virus, lockdown, lost love, failed relationships and more
than the odd political and social commentary that lays it on the line.

This is no nonsense, powerful poetry, written to be spoken, not shouted
from a podium, maybe at speaker's corner to get attention or from be-
hind a news desk, because folks what's here is real, it's happening and
we have a responsibility to listen, understand and act."
Carl Butler (Dark Poetry Society)

In Shadows
ISBN:979-8448585333

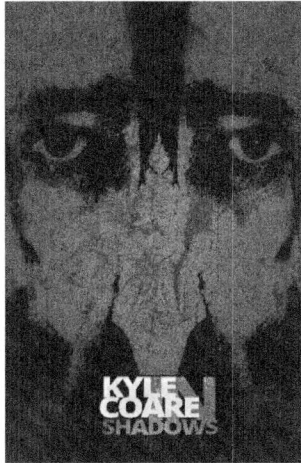

"Something is coming,
its hiding in the dark.
In shadows, it is stalking,
ready to stop your heart"

This poetry collection will take you deep into the bowels
of hell, Through its lava filled mouth, where demons howl.
217 pages of horror themed poetry storytelling.
Filled with humour, scares, light and shade.

"Kyle has once again left us spellbound and on the edge of our seats
with this tantalizing collection. The various forms of proses and poetry
take us through the innermost workings of the unexpected ride that is
life. Your mind and soul will dance in grace and reverie, as you move
through its pages. This incredible title is immersive, in every aspect.

"In Shadows" is an exquisitely crafted masterpiece — a micro adventure
that is a delight to experience; don't delay! If you're looking for material
built with genuine care that can offer soft introspection and the thrill of
discovery, this latest treasure from Kyle is the book for you!"
Realistic Poetry International

Torn Pages: Scraps of midnight
ISBN: 979-8375840512

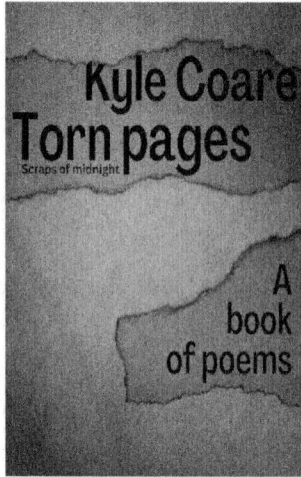

"I bleed internally
from invisible scars.
I want to scream so loudly
I shatter the stars"

Torn Pages is a collection of poems, ripped from the heart, torn from the soul and cut from the mind of poet/author Kyle Coare. Each of the 100+ poems takes you deep into different aspects of life, from love and pain to health and hope. Also touching on struggles with mental health, loss and with society as a whole, whilst always trying to remain playful.

"Any poet this consistent with their skills is destined for greatness!"
Experience the soulful power and journey into the depths of life's emotion through heartfelt words. Feel pain, love, hope and even learn to accept yourself with this honest & raw collection of poems. Let these pages become your silent companion as you discover healing and acceptance with every line.
Torn Pages is absolutely a beautiful piece of work. It's a dreamy, enchanting exploration into a broken world. The poems draw you in and you feel like you are a part of the journey. Torn Pages is definitely worth every penny, it will stay with us for a long time. We've been reading this amazing book all day and we can't seem to put it down!!"
Realistic Poetry International

ABOUT THE AUTHOR

Kyle coare is a poet and author from Leicester, England.
His work veers between enchanting beauty and dark nightmares. Bringing new worlds to life, be they horror landscapes, or dreamy hideaways.
He likes to combine storytelling and poetry, often pointing a spotlight on the world we inhabit. With some humour and some dark edges but is just as comfortable writing about love and hope, as he is loss and hurt. His work can be dark, but through the darkness there is always light.
He has performed at various spoken word events and slams and was the 2022 2funky/Some-Antics slam winner.
His work has also feature on the BBC website.

A Severe
Case of
Writer's Blog

www.facebook.com/wordsandfluff
Https://linktr.ee/wordsandfluff